YOUR LIFE IS EVERLASTING

LET IT MAKE A DIFFERENCE!

Publisher: Romain Lizé
Editors: David Gabillet, Fleur Nabert-Valjavec, Claire Stacino
Layout: Gauthier Delauné
Iconography: Isabelle Mascaras
Proofreading: Alexi Sargeant
Production: Thierry Dubus and Marie Dubourg
Photo-engraving: Les Caméléons
Translation: Lauren Butler-Bergier and Janet Chevrier
Mastering: José Gurdak – Cristal Music

www.magnificat.com

- PIERRE-MARIE DUMONT -

YOUR LIFE IS EVERLASTING

LET IT MAKE A DIFFERENCE!

A spiritual journey into the Mystery of Salvation
with prayer, music, and drama

MAGNIFICAT®

Paris • New York • Oxford • Madrid • Warsaw

TABLE OF CONTENTS

PROLOGUE 9

INTRODUCTION 12

    The day before the retreat 14

    The structure of each hour 15

    Theme of the day 15

    Introduction 15

    Sign of the cross 15

    Musical prayer of the heart 15

        How to pray to music 15

    Reading from the Word of God 17

        How to read the Word of God 17

    Meditation 18

        What posture should you adopt? 19

        How to meditate 19

    Musical prayer of hope 20

    The Mystery 22

    Silent contemplation 23

    Our Father 26

    Closing prayer 26

    How to experience the retreat together, with your spouse 27

    Opening prayer 30

THE HOUR FOR THE FIRST DAY: THE MYSTERY OF EVIL 33

    Introduction 33

    Sign of the cross 34

    Musical prayer of the heart: *Miserere Mei, Deus* 34

    Reading from the Word of God 37

    Meditation 39

    Musical prayer of hope: *Veni Sancte Spiritus* 40

    The Mystery: The mystery of evil 42

    Silent contemplation 48

    Our Father 50

    Closing prayer 50

THE HOUR FOR THE SECOND DAY: THE TRIUMPH OF MERCY 53

Introduction 53

Sign of the cross 54

Musical prayer of the heart: *Chorus of the Hebrew Slaves* 54

Reading from the Word of God 57

Meditation 59

Musical prayer of hope: *Rorate Caeli desuper* 60

The Mystery: The triumph of mercy 63

Silent contemplation 68

Our Father 70

Closing prayer 70

THE HOUR FOR THE THIRD DAY: THE TRIUMPH OF HUMILITY 75

Introduction 75

Sign of the cross 76

Musical prayer of the heart: *Magnificat* 76

Reading from the Word of God 80

Meditation 83

Musical prayer of hope: *Canticle of the Beatitudes* 84

The Mystery: The triumph of humility 86

Silent contemplation 92

Our Father 94

Closing prayer 94

THE HOUR FOR THE FOURTH DAY: THE MYSTERY OF COMPASSION 97

Introduction 97

Sign of the cross 98

Musical prayer of the heart: *Third Lesson of Tenebrae* 98

Reading from the Word of God 101

Meditation 103

Musical prayer of compassion: *Stabat Mater* 104

The Mystery: The mystery of compassion 108

Silent contemplation 110

Our Father 112

Closing prayer 112

THE HOUR FOR THE FIFTH DAY: THE TRIUMPH OF THE HUMAN BODY........115

Introduction........115

Sign of the cross........116

Musical prayer of the heart: *Exsultet*........116

Reading from the Word of God........123

Meditation........125

Musical prayer of hope: *Ave Verum Corpus*........126

The Mystery: The triumph of the human body........128

Silent contemplation........134

Our Father........136

Closing prayer........136

THE HOUR FOR THE SIXTH DAY: THE TRIUMPH OF THE NEW COMMANDMENT........139

Introduction........139

Sign of the cross........140

Musical prayer of the heart: *Abide with Me*........140

Reading from the Word of God........142

Meditation........145

Musical prayer of hope: *Ubi Caritas*........146

The Mystery: The triumph of the new commandment........148

Silent contemplation........154

Our Father........156

Closing prayer........156

THE HOUR FOR THE SEVENTH DAY: LOVE'S FINAL TRIUMPH........159

Introduction........159

Sign of the cross........160

Musical prayer of the heart: *Libera me*........160

Reading from the Word of God........163

Meditation........165

Musical prayer of hope: *In Paradisum*........166

The Mystery: Love's final triumph........168

Silent contemplation........176

Our Father........178

Closing prayer........178

AFTER YOUR RETREAT... 181

DIES IRAE 182

PRACTICAL CONSIDERATIONS 187

  How to organize you retreat 187

    When to schedule your retreat 187

    Finding the right time of day 187

    Being in good shape 188

    Choosing the right setting 188

    In the outdoors? 189

    Relax and focus 189

    Maintaining your concentration 190

CREDITS 192

  Audio credits 192

  Art credits 193

  Text credits 195

YOUR LIFE IS EVERLASTING: LET IT MAKE A DIFFERENCE!

WHEN WE THINK ABOUT THE ULTIMATE MEANING of our existence, we can never see the forest for a single tree.

Death is the tree that distracts all of our attention.

Death keeps us from seeing, in the fullness of its meaning, the awe-inspiring fact that God created us to be eternal. And just because human beings have become mortal does not mean that they are no longer destined for eternity.

We are forever full of life, and nothing, and no one, will ever put an end to this life. Not ourselves, not Satan, not God himself. At the most, God could bring about the end of time and annihilate the visible universe, which would stop the procreation of all new human beings (cf. the allegorical tale of the Flood). That would not stop all the human beings already created—you and I, among others—from continuing to live outside of time, eternally.

Therefore we begin with the certainty that our existence is everlasting as we learn how to live... and how to die.

Our eternal existence began in time, on the day we were conceived, and we should be fully aware that it will know no end. God's creating design was for our life to continue into eternity, after the end of time, by being "adopted" through love into the Divine Life, for the sake of our own unending happiness.

THE GREAT MYSTERY OF THE TRIUMPH OF EVIL

Alas, our humanity has caught the disease of sin, and sin is radically incompatible with Divine Life. Therefore, evil and its corollary, suffering—and even its very triumph, death—have mysteriously become, to our own misery, the unavoidable prospects of human destiny, even though our existence is not completely subject to evil's power.

Forever?

We can be certain of one thing: God, who is Love, did not create the conditions for our misery. Evil, suffering, and death are antithetical to the benevolent design of his creation.

How did Satan, the Prince of Darkness, succeed in becoming *"the prince of this world,"* as Jesus calls him (John 16:11)? How was the devil able to bring out of Creation an evil dominion? A dominion that has come, to a certain extent, to control human beings, making them, like the demons, rebels against God? This mystery is as bottomless as it is terrifying. Nothing has been revealed about it, aside from the fact itself. It is mentioned, above all, in the story of how Eve was seduced by the Serpent and our first parents were chased out of paradise and, more explicitly, by many teachings in the New Testament, particularly on the Last Judgment.

What has clearly been revealed to us—and Jesus Christ insists on it often—is that our death does not mean we cease to be eternal beings. But, alas, it may seem so, since our death seems to mean that evil has triumphed...

Here, then, is the question above all other questions: has our destiny become one of separation from God, which would mean living eternally under the power of the one who holds dominion over death; in other words, under the power of Satan?

If God does not save us, the answer is yes.

IT IS ABSOLUTELY NECESSARY THAT HUMANITY BE SAVED

Thus, it is not enough for us to dread our death because it is the inescapable, final stop on the voyage of our earthly life. It would be a lesser evil for our existence to end there. We dread our temporal death; it frightens us desperately, because it could mean that our existence has been radically corrupted by evil and that it has been given over to the power of Satan for eternity.

We must become conscious of the unavoidable nature of these anxieties in order to recognize that it is absolutely necessary that humanity be saved. And not so that we may understand—for it is incomprehensible!—but so that we may be able to contemplate, through faith, the earth-shattering means our God and Father has chosen to defeat evil and the powers of death for he has defeated them! through love, and only through love—for he cannot use any other means.

Then, and only then, thanks to the definitive victory of God's love for us, will we no longer fear death; it will only be a "passover" on the way to eternal life, a baptism that will allow us to pass from this world into the arms of our heavenly Father, having been delivered from evil forever.

So, what, then, is the goal of this book and the journey it offers?

To rediscover that, despite our certain death, we do not have two lives to live.

Our eternal life began the day we came into the world.

Our life, here below and in the great beyond, is one.

And so:

- Living a Christian life is already living your eternal life;
- Living a Christian life is already living in God's own life;
- Living a Christian life is being "commissioned" Savior of the world, as a member of the Body of Christ;
- Living a Christian life is living in the graceful trajectory of an invincible hope in our eternal life in heaven.

Pierre-Marie Dumont

ETERNAL... OR ETERNAL?

The first meaning of the word "eternal" is "that which is outside time, with neither a beginning nor an end." Since creatures have a beginning in time, God alone can be said to be eternal.

However, the adjective "eternal" can also be used in its literary sense: "that which is without end, which will never stop existing." This definition takes into account the fact that, after our death, we are destined to join eternity, through participation in the fullness of divine life, for a life outside of time that will have no end.

INTRODUCTION

THIS BOOK IS AN INVITATION TO JOURNEY into the sublime embrace of God's love.

We invite you to experience this book as a seven-hour retreat (see below for recommended structure, and page 187 for practical recommendations) or the pace that best suits you.

It will always be your responsibility to make your own honey by gathering pollen from all the flowers, each one more beautiful and more rich than the last, which have been proposed here. But you're responsible for producing your own honey. To that end, don't let the techniques and efforts used obscure the goal; don't risk coming away from this retreat with a poor harvest.

This retreat will unfold over the course of seven days.

If you cannot avoid it, you may skip a day, or even a weekend, without taking time for the retreat. But be careful not to spread your seven retreat days over more than ten calendar days.

On each of the seven days, you should set aside, separate from the rest of your day, a period of a little less than an hour, which we will refer to here as an "Hour." That Hour will be devoted to the retreat and its preparation. The retreat will have no direct impact on the way you organize the rest of your day.

The retreat itself will last an hour each day during seven days.

The practical guidelines found page 187 primarily aim to help you place yourself in a state of attentive concentration, which will allow you to draw the most benefit from your retreat and open yourself to the action of God's grace.

....

LIKE A MOUNTAIN RACE...

....

It is appropriate to compare this retreat to a mountain race. From the very beginning of the retreat, we will traverse terrain where everything will seem foggy, moments in the desert of tiredness and, for some, of discouragement, without yet coming to see the magnificent vistas we hope for. That is when we must hold on tighter: reread the advice that has been given to us here; get ourselves back together and never give up;

continue, despite everything, moving forward and going higher. We will not regret the efforts we have made when, all of a sudden, we will leave the desert or the fog, and everything will become more clear.

The Hours of this retreat are not meant merely as time spent in pleasant leisure, of the high cultural and spiritual variety. This is a true retreat. It is a retreat, at once exciting and exacting, whose goal is to help you to be raised up into the contemplation of the highest mysteries that touch our common destiny and our purpose in life.

A retreat dedicated to the contemplation of the mysteries of salvation merits a total and profound investment: only under this condition will it bear fruit. This retreat may reveal to what extent we are dependent upon the superficial rhythm of our modern life. This "detoxification" may engender a certain amount of suffering. But it may also reveal itself to be an excellent occasion to form ourselves, in a way that is at the same time practical and relational, to do things in a more profound and enduring manner.

To be able to maintain the spirit of the retreat, the most important rule to follow is never to rush. To proceed as we normally do would already be to progress a little too quickly. Going fast will always be going too fast. We are not trying to beat a speed record from the valley to the summit. We are going to the summit in order to be made richer, along the journey, by the most beautiful of experiences, and not in order to get past them as quickly as we possibly can!

We must take our time, as peacefully as possible, as we read the passages, as we go from one step to another, as we chew, taste, reflect, contemplate, tarry over a passage that particularly moves us or bothers us. All the while, we should never hesitate to take little breaks, when necessary.

THE DAY BEFORE THE RETREAT

On the day before beginning the retreat, you will begin to prepare yourself:

- ▸ by a more substantial and intentional prayer life;
- ▸ by turning your attention to the great questions of existence;
- ▸ by imposing a certain frugality upon yourself in the way you use the goods of this world, beginning with food and entertainment (movies, television, internet, social networks, etc.);
- ▸ by adopting a certain seriousness in your thoughts, your conversations, your interests.

Among other things, in order to begin preparing yourself, you will choose a good time to sit down in a calm place and listen to Verdi's *Dies Irae* (CD 1, tracks 1 to 10, about 35 minutes). Do not necessarily try to follow the music precisely alongside the text in Latin (you will find this on page 183). You must, however, find the beginning of each of the ten couplets, the first words of which have been printed in bold. It is important to let the text sink in, all the while letting your spirit move freely with the music.

You will see that the text of the *Dies Irae*, which dates from the Middle Ages, reflects an undeniable terror concerning the end of the world and the Last Judgment. Admittedly, this way of beginning may seem a little rough—particularly when you consider that this is neither the subject matter, nor the goal of the retreat. However, even as you keep in mind the mentality of the century in which this text was written, you should nonetheless prepare for the retreat by contemplating Christ's inescapable return. You may also reconnect with what was once an intense awareness of the gravity of sin, as well as of the seriousness of human existence.

THE STRUCTURE OF EACH HOUR

THEME OF THE DAY

Each day, the retreat time opens with a title that reveals the mystery you will contemplate on that day. Spend some time with this title, asking questions about what it evokes for you, especially in relation to your own spiritual experience.

INTRODUCTION

Under the heading of the mystery, the introduction situates this retreat Hour within salvation history, from the point of view of revelation as well as its potential relationship to your own life.

It should be read with great care to give you a solid point of reference for what follows.

➢ If need be, you may reread, and attempt to connect to your own inner life, any passage that seems obscure, provocative, or particularly meaningful. You could copy it down in your notepad and return to it later over the course of the retreat.

SIGN OF THE CROSS

After reading the Introduction, each Hour begins with the sign of the cross, made slowly while saying aloud: "In the name of the Father, and of the Son, and of the Holy Spirit. Amen."

After the sign of the cross, the Opening Prayer, based on Saint Thomas Aquinas, is recited (see page 30).

MUSICAL PRAYER OF THE HEART

You will not just be listening to a piece of beautiful sacred music. Above all, you will be praying a text set to music, a remarkable text that touches the soul and puts words to what would otherwise be inexpressible in our supplications to the Lord. So, you must not allow your mind to wander in the reverie of an enlightened classical music enthusiast.

How to pray to music

You must adopt an inner disposition that will allow you, in your inmost self, to hear how the sublime words of the text truthfully respond to the sublime notes of the music.

It is therefore appropriate to focus on the words as they are sung in the work in question. Most of the texts are in Latin, one is in Italian (*Va pensiero*), and one is in French. These texts are accompanied by an English translation. Following along as you listen to the music is a little more complicated than if all the texts were in English, but no more so than following a Latin hymn in your hymnal at Sunday Mass.

The secret is to follow carefully the text in Latin as it is sung. That should be your top priority. If you get a little lost, go back to the start of each verse, which is normally marked by a short pause. You will become acquainted with the English translation at the same time, but secondarily. With practice, it should not be complicated, since the singing of the text is much slower than the reading.

Once this practice of reading becomes automatic, you will be able to simultaneously focus your mind and heart on the emotion communicated by the music, in conjunction with the deep meaning of the words of the prayer. In a curious way, you will find that the sacred language, even if you do not fully understand it, helps to achieve this symbiosis.

➢ At the end, take a little time to pause in silence. You can use this time to note down passages that particularly struck you. This moment is indicated by the symbol: (🔊) Pause .

....
WHY LATIN PRAYERS?
....

The majority of the *Prayers of the Heart* and *Prayers of Hope* we have proposed are Latin. Three principal reasons determined this choice:

The desire to propose only masterpieces. For thousands of years, the great masterpieces of religious music have been set to texts in sacred languages. Thus, they are difficult to find in English—especially since we seek high quality recordings.

When you pray with these musical masterpieces, which are composed to enhance the beauty of the sacred language, in the end you experience the fact that the atemporal, sacred aspect of the language is more suited to contemplating the eternal dimension of our lives than is language in everyday use, beyond any practical difficulty of accessibility.

In the measured use of sacred language in our prayer today,

there is an added dimension of filial piety toward our fathers in the faith. They have preceded us into eternity, but not without handing down the treasures of their prayer. Making use of these treasures is a way to demonstrate that we are already praying in the Communion of Saints.

READING FROM THE WORD OF GOD

"To contemplate God through his Word is to learn to see the world and our relationship to the world through the eyes of God. His Word itself invites us to ask one final question: what conversion of heart, of mind, and of life does God expect from us?" [1]

How shall we read Holy Scripture in order to achieve this —ultimate—end?

How to read the Word of God

To read the Word of God is to listen to the Lord speaking to us. And silence is a precondition for listening. To really grasp what this means, begin the reading... with a minute of silence, eyes closed. Then, make a gesture of veneration; for example, mark the sign of the cross on the page with your thumb.

First step

First do a brief, silent, and perfectly natural reading of the text, thinking of it as a personal letter sent to you by a friend who only ever wishes you well... and that will always be the case with the inspired Scriptures! You may reread one passage or another which you may not have read properly, or understood well, the first time. At the end of this reading, close your eyes and enter deep within yourself to formulate the main idea it has left with you.

Second step

Do a second reading of the text out loud, as though you were reading it as a Mass lector. It is a question of reading, or, more exactly, of listening to the Word with all your being, and then meditating on how it resonates within your heart. "Thus will your eyes, your mouth, your ears be filled with the Word. Scripture must take flesh within you and pervade your entire being." [2]

1 - Bernadette Mélois, former Editor-in-Chief of the French edition of Magnificat
2 - Sr. Isabelle Lepoutre, o.p.

Third step

Then, take your notepad, for Scripture is read, listened to... and written. Read the text for the third and final time, very slowly, with your pencil in hand. Step by step, try to interiorize what you are reading. Memorize any short passage that particularly moves you. "Do not understand 'memorize' in the didactic or intellectual sense, but rather in the sense of welcoming it cordially, of keeping it in your heart, as Mary did, who kept all these things, pondering them in her heart (Lk 2:19)."[3] In your notepad, write down this passage and any others you would like to return to later, for example, to begin a prayer on a day when you just can't think of anything, or to help get through a difficult moment, to rekindle a more lively faith of joyful hope, or to fan the embers of charity when it is burning low, etc.

Interiorizing your prayer

Pause in silence to gather the fruits of the prayer, the music, and the Word of God. Choose a period of silence, from 1 to 5 minutes, depending on how familiar you are with observing silence. Set a timer for the chosen period so that your contemplation is not disturbed by preoccupations about the time. This period of interiorizing your prayer is marked by the symbol: (🙍) Pause.

MEDITATION

The meditations suggested each day during the retreat are inspired by the "Prayer of the Heart" from the Philokalia, dear to Orthodox Christians. We have taken up the methodical, continuous repetition of a single, short prayer; for example, on the first day of the retreat: "My God, come to my assistance! O Lord, make haste to help me!"

This is a humble way to lift up your heart to the level of the mystery you are contemplating and to focus all of your attention on it, while maintaining your whole being in an attitude of prayer (supplication, thanksgiving, praise). Normally, any distraction, any thought that does not have the prayer itself as its object, must be suppressed. That being said, within the framework of the retreat meditations, do not refrain from contemplating the mystery of the day ahead of time or from experiencing legitimate feelings of the heart before the divine wonders we will have the opportunity to encounter.

3 - *Ibid.*

What posture should you adopt?

- ▸ If you are not already doing so, sit down in a peaceful, quiet spot that is not lit too brightly.
- ▸ If you haven't already done so, unplug your landline and set your cellphone to airplane mode.
- ▸ Seat yourself comfortably in an armchair or a deckchair, in a totally natural and relaxed position, in which you find it easy to keep still. Then fold your hands, fingers intertwined, over your stomach, with your forearms resting on your upper thighs.
- ▸ If you're familiar with any meditation positions, you might prefer to sit on a carpet on the floor, either kneeling, seated on your heels, or seated cross-legged on the ground.

How to meditate

Have your rosary beads ready.

Once you are comfortably settled, let your head drop naturally toward your chest; keep your eyes open without focusing on anything; stare a yard or so in front of you into the void; don't let your gaze wander.

Begin by establishing an inner attitude of peace and recollection; breathe slowly and deeply.

Now, repeat continuously, one hundred times, without rushing, the prayer formula for the day. Mark each repetition with one rosary bead in a decade. Thus, you will go through one hundred beads, i.e., ten decades, or two rosaries. This will take about fifteen minutes.

During this recitation, chase from your mind all your habitual cares and worries. And, even more radically, close the door of your mind to all that is not contemplation of the mystery of the day.

Beginners will notice that, even after only ten repetitions, your mind has already lost concentration on the mystery and begins to dwell on other things that seem more important or more attractive. That's normal at this stage. Refocus your attention by fully concentrating on the meaning of the prayer you're reciting and on the deep significance of each word you speak.

In any event, you must never be discouraged. It's true that some are more naturally adept than others at this exercise. You must simply accept it, and offer up your poverty as a beginner. Stick with it;

accept praying in an imperfect way and, little by little, you'll improve. As with any exercise, and meditation is just that, it's only through practicing with perseverance that you will attain the desired level.

First phase

For the first two decades, begin reciting out loud, with your eyes open. Insist on clearly articulating each word with your lips, like an actor trying to make himself heard in the balconies. Try to concentrate all the attention of your mind, then of your heart, on the meaning of these words.

Second phase

During the next three decades, with your eyes half opened, continue the recitation, but this time in a lowered voice, in a whisper, still without rushing.

Focus all your attention, in your mind and then in your heart, on the deep meaning of the words you are speaking.

Third phase

During the last five decades (the second rosary), close your eyes and continue the recitation either in a whisper or silently to yourself. Everyone can choose the manner best suited to them. You can then begin recalling one thing that particularly struck you during the musical prayer of the heart or during the reading from the Word of God. Then another thing, when the moment seems right, that is, when you arrive at a point of prayerfulness corresponding to "I sleep, but my heart keeps watch." All while continuing the recitation, allow your mind free reign, but strictly within the framework of the contemplation of the mystery of the day. All other thoughts must be banished.

Once you arrive at a high quality of meditation, should you truly feel the call, you may lengthen the period of the third phase by reciting twenty to fifty additional prayers (two to five decades).

✳ *N.B.* During meditation, those who are already familiar with the practice may also benefit from a technique of breath control.

MUSICAL PRAYER OF HOPE

The prayers proposed here are magnificent Christian prayers, true treasures of the Tradition. Make them your own through the use of the same technique as that suggested above for the musical

prayer of the heart: first, follow along with the text in Latin as it is sung, then, secondarily but simultaneously, read the English translation.

THE MYSTERY

Along with the Word of God, this is the beating heart of the retreat.

Open yourself up to truly allow the text to captivate you, to be able to immerse yourself in it.

The word "Mystery," as it is used here, has a double meaning. On the one hand, we contemplate the Mystery of the day in a text related to the mystery plays performed in the Middle Ages on the forecourts of cathedrals. On the other hand, we are contemplating a sublime reality, inaccessible to human reason, but of which God offers us a foretaste by revealing himself within human history.

Thus, the Mystery concerns a story deeply inspired by Holy Scripture... and by man's eternal questions about the meaning of life and our purpose.

This text was first written for the stage, and the Mysteries were performed for the Silver Jubilee of MAGNIFICAT at the Kings Theatre, one of the largest theaters in New York, to phenomenal acclaim. See http://www.magnificatday.com/brooklyn.

This text will open you to unforeseen spiritual horizons!

However, you will only fully access it by making the effort of a slow and thoughtful reading, following the cadence of the text as suggested by the typography. Above all, it is essential that you clearly grasp the meaning and the import of what you are reading.

Here or there throughout the reading, don't hesitate to:

- take a short, silent break to refocus your attention and/or to meditate on a particularly moving word;
- reread a passage to better savor its richness;
- note down any sentence to rediscover later.

➢ When your retreat is over, on the eighth day or a little later, outside of the framework of the retreat, you might benefit from briefly rereading the seven mysteries.

SILENT CONTEMPLATION

A work of art, chosen for its exceptional beauty and truth, focuses our attention on the Mystery that has just been read.

Select a period of silence, between 3 and 5 minutes, depending on how used you are to observing silence.

Set your timer to the chosen period so that your quality of contemplation is not disturbed by concerns about the time.

Enter into silence as you contemplate the proposed work of art.

Then, allow your memory to make the connection with the Mystery that has just been read. Savor, ponder, and deepen the thoughts your memory suggests regarding that Mystery.

When your recollection of the essence of the text of the Mystery is well engaged, close your eyes to heighten the quality of interiorization.

➢ You could also write down in your notepad the fruit of this contemplation, or note a few passages that particularly touched you.

THE IMPORTANCE OF ALLOWING YOURSELF PERIODS OF SILENCE

A period of silence is indispensable for understanding, admiring, contemplating, savoring, and letting the beauty of a text, prayer, or work of art enter into your being.

Silence is, essentially, granting your memory permission to express itself in a resonant torrent, like great organ pipes thundering under the vaults of a Romanesque cathedral.

Preoccupied by the pressurized tyranny of our daily activities and amusements, we rarely give our memory the right to speak. And yet it is our memory that digests and makes sense of all the information we constantly take in. If we do not leave ourselves periods of silence to allow our memory to give voice to what it has understood, we end up only retaining, or understanding, what is superficial.

**The Seven Mysteries
of Salvation,**
a symphonic meditation
in two acts performed
on October 6, 2018,
at Brooklyn's Kings Theatre
to mark MAGNIFICAT's
Silver Jubilee.

OUR FATHER

The translation used here is taken directly from the Gospel of Saint Matthew.

In the context of this contemplation of the mysteries of Salvation, this more literal translation seemed particularly interesting, especially in its use of "test" and "evil one."

Reading, rather than reciting from memory, will help you to rethink and reappropriate this prayer which the Savior himself taught us; it is both extraordinary and overwhelming that, forming one voice and one heart with Christ, we may address God as "our Father."

CLOSING PRAYER

This section is to be read very slowly and with great attention, carefully separating all of the successive and complementary ideas from each other.

Don't forget that this is a prayer. You must therefore pray it effectively, personally, and with all your heart, in a spirit of praise, supplication, and thanksgiving

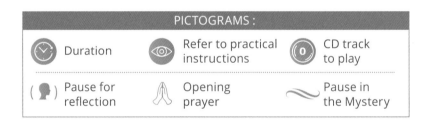

PICTOGRAMS :		
Duration	Refer to practical instructions	CD track to play
Pause for reflection	Opening prayer	Pause in the Mystery

HOW TO EXPERIENCE THE RETREAT TOGETHER, WITH YOUR SPOUSE

Please refer to the chapter "The structure of each Hour" (page 15).

If you and your spouse would like to experience this retreat together, you may adapt the general instructions already provided as follows:

- Have two books, two notepads, and two pens at your disposal.
- The spouses will take turns leading the Hours.
- Before the Hour, the leader for that day will prepare the room, the small table, two comfortable chairs, a candle, the notepads and pens, the two books, the audio system, etc.
- Throughout the Hour, it is the spouse chosen for that day who takes the lead.
- The spouses sit at the table facing each other.

Important: Throughout the prayers, be careful to replace "I" with "we," and "my" with "our," in order to express how your lives are completely united to each other. Although there are two of you, you pray together with one heart, one soul, and one mind.

OPENING

To be read aloud, slowly and solemnly, by the leading spouse. During this, the other spouse silently follows along in his or her book.

SIGN OF THE CROSS

You will make the sign of the cross, and speak it aloud, together.

OPENING PRAYER

Change "me" or "my" to "we" and "our".

MUSICAL PRAYERS OF THE HEART AND OF HOPE

The leading spouse plays the piece of music.

Each of you will experience both of these prayers individually, following along in your own book.

A READING FROM THE WORD OF GOD

First step:

Each of you will do the reading individually and in silence, each respecting the time the other requires.

Second step:

The spouse who is not leading on that day will proclaim the reading aloud, slowly and with good diction.

Third step:

Each of you will do this last step (see page 18) individually, each respecting the time the other requires.

MEDITATION

First and second phases:

During the first five decades (fifty recitations), the Hour's formula of prayer will be recited continually, in a low but audible voice, the first half by the leading spouse, the second half by the other spouse.

> Example:
> Leading spouse: *"Our God, come to our assistance!"*
> Other spouse: *"O Lord, make haste to help us!"*

Each of you may thus take part in the unity of your prayer, in a complementary way.

Third phase:

Each of you will experience the last five decades (50 recitations) individually (see page 20) and in silence, each respecting the time the other requires.

MYSTERY

Each of you will do the reading individually and in silence, each respecting the time the other requires.

SILENT CONTEMPLATION

The leading spouse proposes its length (3 to 5 minutes) and sets a timer.

To be experienced individually, each with your own book.

Both of you stand. One spouse approaches and faces the leading spouse. You join hands and together recite the Our Father aloud.

At the end of the Our Father, you may kiss each other before letting go of each other's hands.

CONCLUSION

Both of you return to your places and sit down.

The leading spouse reads the closing prayer aloud, slowly and solemnly.

During this reading, the other spouse silently follows along in his or her book.

OPENING PRAYER

Spirit of God,
Communion of Love,
Bestower of Wisdom,
Source of All Light:
throughout this Hour,
deign to open my spirit
and illumine my heart;

give me
the presence to contemplate,
the keenness to understand,
the lucidity to interpret
the meaning of these mysteries for meditation;

inspire the beginning of my retreat,
accompany its progress,
crown its end,
and make it bear abundant fruit.
Amen.

DAY 1

THE MYSTERY OF EVIL

After he created the universe, visible and invisible,
God saw that it was good.
After he created mankind,
man and woman, in his image and in his likeness,
God saw that it was very good.
And yet, from the cosmic confines of the universe
to the most intimate place in the human heart,
all of Creation
seems to have come under the power of evil's dominion.
Does that mean I will be miserable, for all eternity?

In the name of the Father,
and of the Son,
and of the Holy Spirit.
Amen.

( ) Recite the opening prayer, p. 30

MUSICAL PRAYER
OF THE HEART

....

MISERERE MEI, DEUS
Allegri

....

ALLEGRI'S *MISERERE* IS A MUSICAL SETTING OF PSALM 50. Composed under the pontificate of Urban VIII, it is unique in having long been sung exclusively in the Sistine Chapel and solely during matins on Holy Wednesdays and Good Fridays. At the end of the office of Tenebrae, as the candles lighting the chapel were extinguished one by one, before the kneeling pope and cardinals, the chapel cantors would improvise elaborate ornamentations of the psalmody. Legend has it that anyone who tried to make public the musical score would be excommunicated on the spot. However, a young boy of fourteen heard it one Holy Wednesday in 1770 and transcribed the music later that night. After a second hearing on Good Friday that same week, he managed to memorize the entire score and began, from that day, to reveal its supreme beauty to the world. That boy was Wolfgang Amadeus Mozart.

....

 12 minutes | How to pray to music - p. 15 | (1) Track 11

....

Miserere mei, Deus, secundum magnam misericordiam tuam.
Have mercy on me, O God, according to your merciful love;

Et secundum multitudinem miserationum tuarum, dele iniquitatem meam.
according to your abundant mercy blot out my transgressions.

Amplius lava me ab iniquitate mea, et peccato meo munda me.
Wash me thoroughly from my iniquity, and cleanse me from my sin!

Quoniam iniquitatem meam ego cognosco, et peccatum meum contra me est semper.
For I know my transgressions, and my sin is ever before me.

Tibi soli peccavi, et malum coram te feci, ut justificeris in sermonibus tuis, et vincas cum judicaris.
Against you, you only, have I sinned, and done that which is evil in your sight,
so that you are justified in your sentence and blameless in your justice.

Ecce enim in iniquitatibus conceptus sum, et in peccatis concepit me mater mea.
Behold, I was brought forth in iniquity, and in sin did my mother conceive me.

Ecce enim veritatem dilexisti, incerta et occulta sapientiae tuae manifestasti mihi.
Behold, you desire truth in the inward being; therefore teach me wisdom in my secret heart.

Asperges me, hyssopo, et mundabor; lavabis me, et super nivem dealbabor.
Purge me with hyssop, and I shall be clean; wash me, and I shall be whiter than snow.

Auditui meo dabis gaudium et laetitiam: et exsultabunt ossa humiliata.
Make me hear joy and gladness; let the bones which you have broken rejoice.

Averte faciem tuam a peccatis meis, et omnes iniquitates meas dele.
Hide your face from my sins, and blot out all my iniquities.

Cor mundum crea in me, Deus, et spiritum rectum innova in visceribus meis.
Create in me a clean heart, O God, and put a new and right spirit within me.

Ne projicias me a facie tua, et spiritum sanctum tuum ne auferas a me.
Cast me not away from your presence, and take not your holy Spirit from me.

Redde mihi laetitiam salutaris tui, et spiritu principali confirma me.
Restore to me the joy of your salvation, and uphold me with a willing spirit.

Docebo iniquos vias tuas, et impii ad te convertentur.
Then I will teach transgressors your ways, and sinners will return to you.

Libera me de sanguinibus, Deus, Deus salutis meae, et exsultabit lingua mea justitiam tuam.
Deliver me from bloodguilt, O God, O God of my salvation,
and my tongue will sing aloud of your deliverance.

Domine, labia mea aperies, et os meum annuntiabit laudem tuam.
O Lord, open my lips, and my mouth shall show forth your praise.

Quoniam si voluisses sacrificium, dedissem utique, holocaustis non delectaberis.
For you take no delight in sacrifice; were I to give a burnt offering, you would not be pleased.

Sacrificium Deo spiritus contribulatus; cor contritum, et humiliatum, Deus, non despicies.
The sacrifice acceptable to God is a broken spirit; a broken and contrite heart,
O God, you will not despise.

Benigne fac, Domine, in bona voluntate tua Sion, ut aedificentur muri Jerusalem.
Do good to Zion in your good pleasure; rebuild the walls of Jerusalem,

Tunc acceptabis sacrificium justitiae, oblationes, et holocausta;
then you will delight in right sacrifices, in burnt offerings and whole burnt offerings;

Tunc imponent super altare tuum vitulos.
then bulls will be offered on your altar.

(🗣) Pause

A READING FROM
THE WORD OF GOD

THE LETTER OF SAINT PAUL TO THE ROMANS 7:15, 17-20, 24a

 How to read the Word of God - p. 17

I do not understand my own actions.

For I do not do what I want, but I do the very thing I hate.

So then it is no longer I that do it,

    but sin which dwells within me.

For I know that nothing good dwells within me, that is, in my flesh.

I can will what is right, but I cannot do it.

For I do not do the good I want,

    but the evil I do not want is what I do.

Now if I do what I do not want,

    it is no longer I that do it, but sin which dwells within me.

Wretched man that I am!

 Pause

MEDITATION

 15 minutes | How to meditate - p. 19

Prayer to repeat continuously

"My God, come to my assistance! O Lord, make haste to help me!"

MUSICAL PRAYER
OF HOPE

....

VENI SANCTE SPIRITUS

....

THE *VENI SANCTE SPIRITUS* IS A GREGORIAN SEQUENCE, attributed to Innocent III (pope from 1198 to 1216), which bears the lovely name "the golden sequence." Its words, simple yet irreplaceable, have been passed down through the centuries from the Middle Ages to our day without losing any of their sense of the luminous mystery of the Holy Spirit. Always chanted at the Mass of the Solemnity of Pentecost, the sequence has been a source of inspiration for the greatest composers, including Josquin des Prez, Orlande de Lassus, and even Mozart. The heavenly beauty of the Gregorian original, however, remains unsurpassed.

....

 3 minutes | How to pray to music - p. 15 | Track 12

....

Veni, Sancte Spiritus, et emitte caelitus lucis tuae radium.
Come, Holy Spirit, come! And from your celestial home, shed a ray of light divine!

Veni, pater pauperum, veni, dator munerum, veni, lumen cordium.
Come, Father of the poor! Come, source of all our store!
Come, within our bosoms shine.

Consolator optime, dulcis hospes animae, dulce refrigerium.
You, of comforters the best; you, the soul's most welcome guest;
sweet refreshment here below;

In labore requies, in aestu temperies, in fletu solatium.
in our labor, rest most sweet; grateful coolness in the heat; solace in the midst of woe.

O lux beatissima, reple cordis intima tuorum fidelium.
O most blessed Light divine, shine within these hearts of yours,
and our inmost being fill!

Sine tuo númine, nihil est in homine, nihil est innoxium.
Where you are not, we have naught, nothing good in deed or thought,
nothing free from taint of ill.

Lava quod est sordidum, riga quod est aridum, sana quod est saucium.
Heal our wounds, our strength renew; on our dryness pour your dew;
wash the stains of guilt away.

Flecte quod est rigidum, fove quod est frigidum, rege quod est devium.
Bend the stubborn heart and will; melt the frozen, warm the chill;
guide the steps that go astray.

Da tuis fidelibus, in te confidentibus, sacrum septenarium.
On the faithful, who adore and confess you, evermore, in your sevenfold gift descend.

Da virtutis meritum, da salutis exitum, da perenne gaudium.
Give them virtue's sure reward; give them your salvation, Lord;
give them joys that never end.

THE MYSTERY

 about 8 minutes

Read slowly, respecting the rhythm indicated by the typographic layout.
Pause for a few seconds, where you see ⌇.

Dialogue between Eve (representing humanity) and God the Father.

EVE
Where are you, Lord?
Why must my soul seek you
and yet never find you?

What keeps you from visiting me
as on those days in paradise?
Is it possible that Mankind has become
distasteful to you?

O Lord,
remember those days of gladness
when you would walk at daybreak
in the garden of Eden.
Answer me!
Do not hide!
Why do you conceal your face from me?
Why do you treat me as your enemy?

O my God,
without you,
without your loving presence,
our paradise is lost;
our Earth, a vale of tears.
When will you cease to try me so?
Yes, I have sinned.

It is my fault,
my grievous fault, my most grievous fault.
If you will no longer speak to me,
how should I know,
O Sovereign Judge,
what I can do
to redeem my transgression?

What do you expect from me?
Tell me:
what can I do
so you will stop afflicting me in this way?

You whom they call "the good Lord,"
do you take pleasure
in oppressing the work of your hands?
In making us pay for our crimes
for ever and ever?

Why did you sculpt me from the clay?
It would have been better
for me
to have never existed!
You have stripped me of all the reasons
I once had to live.
You have given me every reason
to prefer nothingness to being.

Behold, I cry out, "Help me!"
and my God does not answer me…

Here I am, calling on his love
and his heart is not moved.

GOD THE FATHER
Eve, my poor Eve,
do you believe I would reject
the ancestor of all men?
Do you believe I would reject
the ancestor of the mother of God?
Do you believe I would reject
the ancestor of the Son of God?

EVE
O my God,
how obscure
are these words for me!
Alas,
of murderers and of victims
have I become the ancestor!

But since you can hear me,
answer my questions:
have you become cruel
towards your creatures?
Remember
in Eden
how you showed us,
tender Father,
the benevolent design of your Creation:
Giving us a share
in the communion of your love.
Pleasures for evermore!
Tell me it was truly
for this
that you created us!

Tell me, from now on,
are we to fear God, or rather
to love Him? When I lift my thoughts to you

will my mind be filled
with fright?
Or rather, will my heart melt
with love?

GOD THE FATHER
My poor little one!
You know not what you have done
and you know not what you say…
How can you accuse me of your affliction,
although you did not consent
to the Law of your own well-being?

When you speak of me,
you speak as though it were
you
who had created me,
in your own likeness!

I am not the one who is oppressing you,
I am not the one who is entrapping you.

I,
your God and Father,
do not know how to do anything
other than to abide,
a God of mercy and tenderness,
full of love and truth.

Thus, I urge you:
be careful!
Since your Fall,
no one has seen
God:
And so, loving the living and true God
can no longer be,
as it was in Eden,
a movement of the heart towards a loved one,
a dear friend who can be seen,

who is known well,
with whom time can be spent each day,
in real life.
It has become a question of good will:
loving me from now on
is desiring that my will be done
on Earth as it is in Heaven.

EVE
But why?
If you are not the one who is punishing me,
who is the author of my misery?
And if it were I alone
who had to pay the price
of my original fault…
But out of me will come forth
a multitude of peoples.
Generation to generation
all as I am:
subject to imperfection
and at fault;
they will live in enmity
and will kill each other.
All my descendants
will be cast off:
victims and culprits,
culprits and victims;
behold,
they are destined for affliction
and agony.
Death will be, for them,
in the end,
a deliverance to be longed for.

But that is not enough!
Behold,
at the end of a lifetime of pain,
you have destined them
to the outer darkness

where there is weeping and gnashing of teeth
forever.

Does not one miserable existence
suffice to quench
your thirst for justice?

If that is indeed the case,
why then should we continue to be fruitful
and multiply?
Why procreate,
if our children's destiny
is to become heirs to our misery,
without remission?

GOD THE FATHER
Truly, truly, my child,
sin,
your sin,
is the only author of your misery.
Why then accuse me,
I who am your God and Father?

Can you not see?
By your sin,
you have put me,
I who am your Lord and your God,
in some state of powerlessness
before Satan,
who has taken you hostage
with your own cooperation.

Can you understand that?

Although you have betrayed me,
I can never cease loving you.

Although you are in the power of evil,
I cannot cease wanting what is good for you.

It is as though
my Justice and my Omnipotence
were disarmed,
given that,
were they to be exerted,
the price of my victory over evil
would be the condemnation and punishment
of a loved one.

Can you understand that?

EVE
Yes,
for once I can understand you;
was I not made in your image?
You see:
my mother's heart
is unable
to no longer love
even Cain,
he who cut down my favorite son.

GOD THE FATHER
You have discovered
the secret of God:
I am a Father
who loves like a mother.

EVE
Lord,
I am only a weak and limited being.
How can it be
that my crime
should ripple out onto my children,
and onto my children's children,
and that its consequences
could make the foundation

of the visible universe
tremble, and the invisible universe as well,
until it would corrupt
your creating plan,
even in its own benevolence?

GOD THE FATHER
I have said, "You are gods,
and all sons of the Most High!
This begetting word
cannot be abolished.

Through my Only Begotten Son,
my Beloved,
and for him,
I have put in you,
finite beings,
a seed of the Infinite
that cannot be eradicated.

There is the drama of your fall:
your trespass
closes you irremediably in finitude,
although you were predestined
for the Infinite.

Immortal
as well as eternal,
have I created you.
By your sin,
behold, you have become mortal,
but that does not mean
you remain any less
eternal.

By your sin,
you have made it so that time
has made
eternity ill.

EVE
Lord, forgive me
if I am being obtuse,
but again,
everything you are saying
is beyond my comprehension…

GOD THE FATHER
By the grace of Creation,
in my only Son,
through Him
and for Him,
you are destined for the bosom of God.
By this grace,
which is irrevocable,
in every man that sees the daylight,
in every woman who is brought into the world,
I can only recognize,
although disfigured by sin,
I can only recognize,
although he may sneer like a devil,
I can only recognize
one of my children.
Forever,
I can only continue to love
him who is the little brother of my Beloved Son,
her who is the little sister of my Beloved Son.

Alas, three times alas!
Behold how you,
my beloved heirs,
you in whom subsists
forever
the original eucharist of my only Son,
behold how you are in the power of Satan,
the author of sin by hatred of Love.

In you the sap of concupiscence
has been substituted for the sap of Charity;

in you the powers of evil and of death
have corrupted the potential for eternal life.

Now do you understand why?
Why, through the intrusion
of sin into the world,
the very foundation of the Cosmos
has been shaken?

Since my loving plan for Creation
and for adoption
has been repudiated,
it is as though humanity has divorced
its own purpose in life,
without being able to cease to be.

EVE
Lord!
Have pity on us, poor sinners!
Save us!

GOD THE FATHER
What can I do?

I, the Sovereign Good,
can have no part in sin!

And yet!
My Fatherly Love perceives
intensely,
poignantly,
heartbreakingly,
what the consequences of a single sin
can be for you, my children.

O, how
I suffer from the symptoms:

evil, suffering, and death
which, torturing you, rend my Fatherly heart.

My divine heart bleeds
blood and water,
time and time again,
before the wretchedness into which you have
fallen.

And so, no,
your sin does not enflame
the charges of my Justice;
it does not offend
the unalterable perfection
of my Holiness;
it does not defy
my Omnipotence:
it only fans the fire of my Love for you.
As though it were possible to add, to my infinite
perfections,
a supreme perfection,
I, who am the God of love and of tenderness,
have become, because of your sin,
forever,
a God of compassion.

SILENT CONTEMPLATION

 3 to 5 minutes

Set a timer for the chosen period so that the quality of silence
is not affected by concerns about the time.

Adam and Eve
George Frederic Watts
(c. 1865)

OUR FATHER

Our Father in heaven,
holy be your name,
your kingdom come and your will be done,
on earth as in heaven.
Give us today the kind of bread we need.
Forgive us our debts
just as we have forgiven those who are in debt to us.
Do not bring us to the test
but deliver us from the evil one.

CLOSING PRAYER

Master and Creator of all things,
your grace is the only hope we have.
So that we may not doubt that you love us as a father,
when we recognize ourselves as sinners, listen to our humble pleas;
be lenient with us, show us your compassion,
free us from our bad inclinations, orient our lives towards your goodness
and save us from eternal damnation.
Amen.

"God did not make death,
and he does not delight
in the downfall of the living."

Book of Wisdom 1:13

DAY 2

THE TRIUMPH OF MERCY

God is determined to save humanity,

and so he must confront the dominion of Evil and defeat it.

But how is he to make us understand that,

in order to wage this war,

he will not engage the omnipotence of his arm,

but rather, the extreme weakness of his tenderness;

and, even more incomprehensibly,

the Savior he sends us will not be the Most High,

but rather, the lowest of the lowly?

God will therefore elect a people from amongst the nations

and lead it little by little,

through a holy history full of twists and turns,

to share in his unimaginable plan of Salvation,

until the time is accomplished

for it to be manifested to the whole world.

In the name of the Father,
and of the Son,
and of the Holy Spirit.
Amen.

( ) Recite the opening prayer - p. 30

MUSICAL PRAYER
OF THE HEART

....

CHORUS OF THE HEBREW SLAVES
Giuseppe Verdi

....

THE CHORUS OF THE HEBREW SLAVES, commonly known as *Va pensiero,* is one of the most famous choruses in the world, drawn from the third act of the opera *Nabucco* (1842) by Verdi (1813-1901). Inspired by Psalm 136, it is the hymn of hope the Hebrew slaves sing in Babylon, after the destruction of the first Temple of Jerusalem. This "psalm without borders" expresses the pain of captivity but also, consequently, is a magnificent hymn to the liberty which God's mercy will not delay in procuring for his people. The lost and devastated homeland is a figure of Creation vanquished by Satan. The enslavement in Babylon evokes the power of sin that had held humanity in its thrall.

 5 minutes | How to pray to music - p. 15 | ① Track 13

Va, pensiero, sull'ali dorate;
Go, thoughts, on golden wings;

Va, ti posa sui clivi, sui colli,
Go, settle upon the slopes and hills,

Ove olezzano tepide e molli
Where warm and soft and fragrant are

L'aure dolci del suolo natal!
The breezes of our sweet native land!

Del Giordano le rive saluta,
Greet the banks of the Jordan,

Di Sionne le torri atterrate…
The towers of Zion…

Oh mia patria sì bella e perduta!
Oh my country so beautiful and lost!

Oh membranza sì cara e fatal!
Oh so dear yet unhappy!

Arpa d'or dei fatidici vati,
Oh harp of the prophetic seers,

Perché muta dal salice pendi?
Why do you hang silent from the willows?

Le memorie nel petto raccendi,
Rekindle the memories within our hearts,

Ci favella del tempo che fu!
Tell us about the times that have gone by!

O simile di Solima ai fati
Or similar to the fate of Solomon,

Traggi un suono di crudo lamento,
Give a sound of lament;

O t'ispiri il Signore un concento
Or let the Lord inspire a concert

Che ne infonda al patire virtù, (ter)
That may give to endure our suffering,

Al patire virtù!
To endure our suffering!

( ) Pause

A READING FROM THE WORD OF GOD

THE GOSPEL ACCORDING TO SAINT LUKE 1:68-79

 How to read the Word of God - p. 17

The text here is the Benedictus, the prophetic canticle pronounced by Zechariah on the day of his son John's circumcision. The "child" he addresses at the end of the canticle is thus his son, John the Baptist, the last and greatest of the prophets of Israel, who prepared the way of the Lord.

Blessed be the Lord God of Israel,
for he has visited and redeemed his people,
and has raised up a horn of salvation for us
    in the house of his servant David,
as he spoke by the mouth of his holy prophets from of old,
    that we should be saved from our enemies, and from the hand of all who hate us;
to perform the mercy promised to our fathers,
    and to remember his holy covenant,

the oath which he swore to our father Abraham,
    to grant us that we, being delivered from the hand of our enemies,
might serve him without fear, in holiness and righteousness
    before him all the days of our life.

And you, child, will be called the prophet of the Most High;
    for you will go before the Lord to prepare his ways,
to give knowledge of salvation to his people
    in the forgiveness of their sins,
through the tender mercy of our God,
    when the day shall dawn upon us from on high

to give light to those who sit in darkness and in the shadow of death,
    to guide our feet into the way of peace.

 Pause

MEDITATION

 15 minutes | How to meditate - p. 19

Prayer to be repeated continuously

"O come, o come, Emmanuel, and ransom captive Israel."

MUSICAL PRAYER
OF HOPE

RORATE CAELI DESUPER

RORATE CAELI DESUPER IS A TRADITIONAL ADVENT HYMN that takes up a famous passage from the Prophet Isaiah (45:8): "Shower, O heavens, from above, and let the skies rain down righteousness; let the earth open, that salvation may sprout forth, and let it cause righteousness to spring up also; I the LORD have created it." In the past, the Mass known as the Rorate was celebrated in honor of Mary on Saturdays during the Advent season. Owing to the Gospel of the Annunciation of the Lord by the angel Gabriel, it also bore the lovely name of the "Angelic Mass." Its liturgical color was white. At the dawn of a new day, in candlelight, the Church celebrates its Savior. To this day, the beauty of this hymn makes of us "watchers for the dawn."

 5 minutes | How to pray to music - p. 15 | Track 14

℟ *Rorate caeli desuper, et nubes pluant Justum.*
℟ **Drop down dew, ye heavens, from above, and let the clouds rain down the Just One.**

1. Ne irascaris, Domine, ne ultra memineris iniquitatis:
1. Be not angry, O Lord, and remember no longer our iniquity:

ecce civitas Sancti tui facta est deserta,
behold the city of the Holy One is become a desert:

Sion deserta facta est, Jerusalem desolata est,
Sion is become a desert: Jerusalem is desolate:

domus sanctificationis tuae et gloriae tuae, ubi laudaverunt te patres nostri. ℟
the house of thy sanctification and of thy glory, where our fathers praised thee.

2. Peccavimus et facti sumus tamquam immundus omnes nos,
2. We have sinned and are become as one that is unclean:

et cecidimus quasi folium universi
and we have all fallen as a leaf,

et iniquitates nostrae quasi ventus abstulerunt nos:
and our iniquities like the wind have carried us away:

abscondisti faciem tuam a nobis, et allisisti nos in manu iniquitatis nostrae. ℟
thou hast hidden thy face from us, and hast crushed us in the hold of our iniquity.

3. Vide Domine, afflictionem populi tui,
3. Behold, O Lord, the affliction of thy people,

et mitte quem missurus es:
and send forth Him Who is to come:

emitte Agnum dominatorem terrae de petra deserti ad montem filiae Sion,
send forth the Lamb, the ruler of the earth, from the Rock of the desert,
to the mount of daughter Sion:

ut auferat ipse jugum captivitatis nostrae. ℟
that he may take away the yoke of our captivity.

4. Consolamini, consolamini, popule meus: cito veniet salus tua.
4. Be comforted, be comforted, my people: thy salvation cometh quickly:

Quare maerore consumeris, quare innovavit te dolor?
why art thou consumed with grief: for sorrow hath estranged thee: I will save thee:

Salvabo te, noli timore: ego enim sum Dominus Deus tuus,
fear not, for I am the Lord thy God,

Sanctus Israel, Redemptor tuus. ℞.
the Holy One of Israel, thy Redeemer.

THE MYSTERY

 about 5 minutes

Read slowly, respecting the rhythm indicated by the typographic layout.

Dialogue between Israel and God the Father.

GOD THE FATHER
My people, what have I done to you
that you deny me
so?
How have I disappointed you?
Answer me.

I made a holy covenant
with you.
I chose you among the Nations
to be my people,
the people from whom will come forth
the Salvation of the world.

I promised my grace to Abraham,
to Jacob my faithfulness.
And I have kept my promise.

I freed you from slavery in Egypt.
To Moses, I gave a Law
to soften the hardness of your heart
and to prepare you to receive,
when the time has been fulfilled,
the fullness of Salvation.
I set you up in a land of dreams,

Canaan, your inheritance.
And I made of your country
a place for myself,
so that it would become the gateway of
salvation.

I swore my faith to David,
my servant.
I anointed him with my holy oil.

And remember:
when I brought you out of exile in Babylon
to plant you once again within your walls,
you were all as in a dream.

And yet,
again and always,
you do not walk according to my judgments,
you do not keep my commandments,
you profane my precepts,
you deny our Covenant.

ISRAEL
Convert us, O Lord, to you,
and we will be converted.
Renew your love for us,
and we will love you.

GOD THE FATHER

O my people,
I planted you as a choice vineyard
to make the Vine of Salvation
spring up among you.

How did you become
a corrupt wild vine in an alien vineyard?
I expected sweet grapes
and you gave me wild grapes,
bitter indeed.

ISRAEL

O Lord,
do not repudiate your covenant.
Do not take your grace away from us,
for the love of Abraham, your friend,
of Isaac, your servant,
and of Jacob, your holy one!

GOD THE FATHER

My vineyard has been ravaged;
my favorite dwelling has been
trampled underfoot.
Jackals prowl there,
in the shadow of death.
Would I not take this to heart?
Would not this misfortune affect me?

O my vineyard,
your faults are stronger than you are,
but I, your God,
love you more than I despise your faults.

I will forgive what you owe me.
I will cover the price of your sins.
I will come to give you life,
and you will live once more.

Yes, my vineyard,
I love you
without measure.
I will come to save you,
I will say to you:
"Here I am! Here I am!
I am coming!"

ISRAEL

O Lord,
all our sacred history
shows us this:
your love lying in wait,
on the lookout for the slightest opportunity
to prevail over your justice!

GOD THE FATHER

Behold, the days are coming
when I will plant
the Vine of Life
in the center of my vineyard.
He will come forth from the root of Jesse.
Upon him I will graft once again,
first the shoots of Israel,
then the wild seedlings
of the Nations.
And they will come back to life.

Then will my vineyard produce
the golden fruit
I await from her.
And behold:
with her, I will establish a Covenant,
new and eternal.

ISRAEL

Lord,
I recognize your faithfulness:
in our time, make it live again!

I admire your work of salvation:
in our time, accomplish it!

GOD THE FATHER
Behold:
the Redeeming Vine
will bring forth shoots without number.
They will flower.
They will send out twining tendrils
that will attach themselves to each other
through the bond of charity.
In plenty
will they produce
lush branches here below,
bunches of golden grapes in life eternal.

Arise, my vineyard, in splendor!
In you, my glory will arise.
In your midst,
the Uncreated Vine is already springing up.

He will lift up the fallen,
he will straighten those who are bent.

Here he is!
He comes, he in whom I will make
all things new!
Already he rides upon the clouds,
and toward you,
his promised one,
he inclines the heavens.

Here he is, O my vineyard,
your Savior!
Like the rising sun,
he rends the darkness of night.
He will dispel your misfortune.

From the night terrors, you will be delivered.
From your fright, you will be liberated.
From your anguish, he will save you.

He will exalt you.
He will make you see happiness.
He will give you more and more,
more than your heart can desire.

In those days,
you will be radiant.
Your heart will leap
with joy.
It will grow wide with happiness.
For you will see
the Salvation of God take root in you.

Soon,
the nations will graft themselves on you,
and kings will nourish themselves
with your sap.
Lift up your eyes and see:
all the peoples will come to you,
you will bring them all together.

Yes, here HE is, he is coming.
You will see him
with your own eyes,
my Messiah,
your Redeemer!

Behold, the one who is coming
is your God,
himself,
in person.

He is
the one who is Life in me,
from the beginning and forever:
my beloved,
my Son,
my Only Begotten One!

Thus,
all of you,
who were created
in Him and for Him,
will be lifted up
through Him and in Him.

ISRAEL
O my God,
what is humanity
that you should cherish it so?
What is humanity
that you should give your Son
for it?

SILENT CONTEMPLATION

 3 to 5 minutes

Set a timer for the chosen period so that the quality of silence
is not affected by concerns about the time.

*Christ and the Apostles
(I am the Vine)*
Greek School
17th c.

OUR FATHER

Our Father in heaven,
holy be your name,
your kingdom come and your will be done,
on earth as in heaven.
Give us today the kind of bread we need.
Forgive us our debts
just as we have forgiven those who are in debt to us.
Do not bring us to the test
but deliver us from the evil one.

CLOSING PRAYER

God of mercy,

restore your Creation for us,

for without your grace, our life falls into ruin;

do not allow the attractions of this world and the worries of our existence

to obscure that we await the Savior you have promised us;

but rather, awaken in us the intelligence of heart that will prepare us to welcome him;

and may the love we bear those who are close to us

form already, in our daily life,

the love that will allow us to recognize him when he comes.

Amen.

"For my father and my mother
have forsaken me,
but the LORD will take me up."

Psalm 27:10

When ages beyond number had run their course
from the creation of the world,
when God in the beginning created heaven and earth,
and formed man in his own likeness;
when century upon century had passed
since the Almighty set his bow in the clouds
after the Great Flood, as a sign of covenant and peace;
in the twenty-first century since Abraham,
our father in faith, came out of Ur of the Chaldees;
in the thirteenth century since the People of Israel
were led by Moses in the Exodus from Egypt;
around the thousandth year since David was anointed King;
in the sixty-fifth week of the prophecy of Daniel;
in the one hundred and ninety-fourth Olympiad;
in the year seven hundred and fifty-two
since the foundation of the City of Rome;
in the forty-second year of the reign
of Caesar Octavian Augustus,
the whole world being at peace,

Jesus Christ,
eternal God and Son of the eternal Father,
desiring to consecrate the world
by his most loving presence, was conceived
by the Holy Spirit,
and when nine months had passed since his conception,
was born of the Virgin Mary in Bethlehem of Judah,
and was made man:

The Nativity
of Our Lord Jesus Christ
according to the flesh.

DAY 3

THE TRIUMPH OF HUMILITY

So great is God's love for the world
that he sent his Only Son to save us:
behold how he has made his Beloved,
begotten before time, enter time's passing.
He desired that he resemble us in everything, except sin,
so that he might love in us what he loves in him:
we, who left God's covenant through our pride,
return to it through his humility.

In the name of the Father,
and of the Son,
and of the Holy Spirit.
Amen.

( ) Recite the opening prayer - p. 30

MUSICAL PRAYER
OF THE HEART

MAGNIFICAT

Adrian Willaert

BORN IN FLANDERS, Adrian Willaert was trained in Paris and moved to Italy where he became, beginning in 1527, chapel master at the prestigious Saint Mark's Basilica in Venice. Based on the setting of the sixth Gregorian tone (*sexti toni*), this *Magnificat* is a model of clarity and simplicity alternating portions of polyphony with plainchant. It expresses beautifully the joy and the contemplation proper to the hymn of thanksgiving that welled up in the heart of Mary as she greeted Elizabeth (Lk 1:47-55). May each one of us, in our own personal history, carry on salvation history as sung by Our Lady of the Visitation! May the Lord never cease looking down upon our lives and performing great things for us! In this way, the *Magnificat* will rightly become our own personal prayer. More than that, it will become our own prayer for eternal life! The Our Father and the Hail Mary will pass away; the *Magnificat* will never die. For, in blessed eternity, we will no longer have need to ask our Father to deliver us from evil, nor to beg the Mother of God to pray for us at the hour of our death. On the contrary, united in heart with Mary and the Communion of Saints, we will always and ever more have call to sing: "My soul proclaims the greatness of the Lord, my spirit rejoices in God my Savior!"

 6 minutes | How to pray to music - p. 15 | Track 1

Magníficat ánima mea Dóminum,
My soul magnifies the Lord,

Et exultávit spíritus meus: in Deo salutári meo.
and my spirit rejoices in God my Savior,

Quia respéxit humilitátem ancíllae suae:
for he has looked with favor on the lowliness of his servant.

Ecce enim ex hoc beátam me dicent omnes generatiónes.
Surely, from now on all generations will call me blessed;

Quia fécit mihi mágna qui pótens est:
for the Mighty One has done great things for me,

et sánctum nómen eius.
and holy is his name.

Et misericórdia eius a progénie
His mercy is for those who fear him

in progénies timéntibus eum.
from generation to generation.

Fécit poténtiam in bráchio suo:
He has shown strength with his arm;

dispérsit supérbos mente cordis sui.
he has scattered the proud in the thoughts of their hearts.

Depósuit poténtes de sede:
He has brought down the powerful from their thrones,

et exaltávit húmiles.
and lifted up the lowly;

Esuriéntes implévit bonis:
he has filled the hungry with good things,

et dívites dimísit inánes.
and sent the rich away empty.

Suscépit Ísrael púerum suum:
He has helped his servant Israel,

recordátus misericórdiae suae.
in remembrance of his mercy,

Sicut locútus est ad patres nostros:
according to the promise he made to our ancestors,

Ábraham, et sémini eius in saecula.
to Abraham and to his descendants forever.

Glória Patri, et Fílio, et Spirítui Sancto,
Glory be the Father, and to the Son, and to the Holy Spirit,

Sicut erat in princípio, et nunc, et semper,
as it was in the beginning, is now, and ever shall be,

et in sæcula sæculórum.
forever and ever.

Amen.
Amen.

) Pause

A READING FROM
THE WORD OF GOD

LETTER OF SAINT PAUL TO THE EPHESIANS 1:3-14

 How to read the Word of God - p. 17

Blessed be the God and Father of our Lord Jesus Christ,
    who has blessed us in Christ with every spiritual blessing
    in the heavenly places,
    even as he chose us in him before the foundation of the world,
    that we should be holy and blameless before him.
He destined us in love to be his sons through Jesus Christ,
    according to the purpose of his will,
    to the praise of his glorious grace
    which he freely bestowed on us in the Beloved.
In him we have redemption through his blood,
    the forgiveness of our trespasses, according to the riches
    of his grace which he lavished upon us.
For he has made known to us in all wisdom and insight the mystery
    of his will, according to his purpose
    which he set forth in Christ
    as a plan for the fullness of time, to unite all things in him,
    things in heaven and things on earth

In him, according to the purpose
of him who accomplishes all things according to the counsel of his will,
we who first hoped in Christ
have been destined and appointed
to live for the praise of his glory.
In him you also, who have heard the word of truth,
the gospel of your salvation, and have believed in him,
were sealed with the promised Holy Spirit,
which is the guarantee of our inheritance
until we acquire possession of it,
to the praise of his glory.

( ) Pause

MEDITATION

 15 minutes | How to meditate - p. 19

Prayer to repeat continuously

"Lord Jesus Christ, Son of God, have mercy on us sinners!"

MUSICAL PRAYER OF HOPE

....

CANTICLE OF THE BEATITUDES

....

CREATED IN 2006, the Georgian Harmony Choir comprises professionals as well as passionate amateurs, under the direction of its foundress, Nana Peradze, a composer and gifted singer with an exceptional voice, and head of the Saint Symeon Choir of Saint Sava Church, in Paris. The choir here sings the *Canticle of the Beatitudes* in French, set to a traditional Orthodox melody.

The announcement of the Beatitudes (Mt 5:3-12) opens the Sermon on the Mount in which Jesus reveals the secret of eternal happiness. And indeed, we can be happy not only in this world, we are also promised undying happiness in the next. In formulating the Beatitudes, our Savior paints a picture of his earthly life—and bestows it on us!—a life of a true man lived according to the Spirit of the Father, gentle and humble of heart, experiencing and being tested by the sorrows of the world, thirsty for holiness, hungry for justice, compassionate and merciful, pure love and nothing but love, a peacemaker, persecuted for righteousness. In so doing, Jesus describes the incorruptible happiness in which our lives will continue in the hereafter, for, as we identify with his life on earth, so shall we be identified with his eternal divine life, in union with the Father, in the communion of the Spirit of Love.

Thus, the Beatitudes place before us the prospect of invincible hope, but also the decisive choices in our lives on earth.

....

 3 minutes | How to pray to music - p. 15 | Track 2

....

Dans ton Royaume souviens-toi de nous, Seigneur,
In your Kindgom, O Lord, remember us.

Lorsque tu viendras dans ton Royaume.
when you come into your kingdom

Bienheureux les pauvres en esprit car le Royaume des Cieux est à eux.
Happy are the poor in spirit, for theirs is the kingdom of heaven.

Bienheureux les affligés car ils seront consolés.
Happy are those who mourn, for they will be comforted.

Bienheureux les doux car ils hériteront de la terre.
Happy are the meek, for they will inherit the earth.

Bienheureux les affamés et assoiffés de justice, car ils seront rassasiés.
Happy are those who hunger and thirst for righteousness, for they will be filled.

Bienheureux les miséricordieux car ils obtiendront miséricorde.
Happy are the merciful, for they will receive mercy.

Bienheureux les cœurs purs car ils verront Dieu.
Happy are the pure in heart, for they will see God.

Bienheureux les pacificateurs, car ils seront appelés fils de Dieu.
Happy are the peacemakers, for they will be called children of God.

Bienheureux les persécutés pour la justice,
Happy are those who are persecuted for righteousness' sake,

car le Royaume des Cieux est à eux.
for theirs is the kingdom of heaven.

Bienheureux serez-vous lorsqu'on vous outragera, et qu'on vous persécutera,
Happy are you when people revile you and persecute you

et qu'on dira faussement de vous toute sorte de mal à cause de moi.
and utter all kinds of evil against you falsely on my account.

Réjouissez-vous, et soyez dans l'allégresse!
Rejoice and be glad,

car votre récompense sera grande dans les cieux.
for your reward is great in heaven.

THE MYSTERY

ACT III - THE TRIUMPH OF HUMILITY

 about 7 minutes

Read slowly, respecting the rhythm indicated by the typographic layout.
Pause for a few seconds, where you see ∿.

Mary, Mother of God, seated,
with her cousin Elizabeth.

MARY
I am a woman.
A woman about whom
there is not much
to say.

And for the world,
I am,
perhaps,
the least interesting woman
in the world.
They sent me to give birth
in a stable.
There you have it!

For the world,
I am a small young woman
with no prospects,
barely good for making conversation
with an ox and a donkey.

And it is true,
I do not have much to say.
I am a most quiet woman:
I keep everything in my heart
between me and my God.

Nor do I have,
it is true,
much ambition.
I do not particularly care about
succeeding,
giving orders,
becoming important,
envied,
rich,
or famous.

And I am satisfied with depending
upon the love of those who love me.

My happiness?
I have found it
as a woman,
as a wife,
and as a mother,
in the sanctifying prose
of my humble, daily work.

The secret of my happiness?
It is so simple!
In the humblest things of my life,
I contemplate God at work,
as he accomplishes wonders.

A tender gesture;
a smile;

the family meal;
the sound of Joseph's workshop,
the smell of wood
being flattened under the jointer plane;
the silence when my Child falls asleep
after nursing;
all those things from morning
to night which,
in my very simple life,
make God's grace
perceptible and obvious.

You see,
the little happenings
of my life
are what make me
just a humble servant,
as it pleases God.

What fills me with joy
is giving myself
in service to others,
without desiring any other reward
except loving
and knowing that I am loved.

And you see,
being happy
and making others happy
keeps me busy all the time,
because I like everybody,
everyone Providence has brought
close to me.

So it is true,
I am not really
a woman who is interesting
to the world.
And yet, if you knew,

if you could understand me,
see what I keep secret:
an angel came to tell me
that I am a woman blessed
among women,
full of grace...

ELIZABETH
Yes, Mary,
I cherish you as though
you were my own daughter,
and I can bear witness:
you are blessed among women,
and Jesus, your Child, is blessed.
You were the purest of newborns,
the only one who was completely pure,
in truth.
And then, you were the sweetest little girl
in the world,
as well as the most helpful.
and you were the prettiest of maidens
in the bloom of youth,
as well as the most chaste.
And you were the loveliest fiancée
in the world,
as well as the most reliable.
And now you are the most loving of wives,
because you are the most beloved, as well.
May God bless Joseph, your spouse.

MARY
And I am the happiest of mothers:
the most fulfilled,
the most full of wonder,
the most thankful,
the most devoted;
the most consecrated
of mothers.

Through my dear husband,
and, as though over-abundantly,
through my dear Child,
I am a blessed woman,
I am a woman full of grace.

I told you, I do not speak much,
only when I have something vital
to say—
a *Magnificat,*
for example:
My soul proclaims the greatness of the Lord,
my spirit rejoices in God, my Savior!

Now,
for you who are listening to me,
today,
I would like to continue my canticle
of thanksgiving,
by telling you:
how beautiful it is to be a woman,
a woman according to God's heart!

How beautiful it is to be a woman,
a happy woman,
in the vocation where God's plan has
personally
chosen her, elected her,
consecrated her.

Yes,
how beautiful it is to be a woman
for whom,
in whom,
with whom,
the Almighty does great things.

Yes, how beautiful it is to be a woman,
free,
because she has been freed from sin,
by the grace of God!

O, I beseech you, when,
for some extraordinary reason,
I speak,
as I am speaking here, today,
would you be so good as to listen to me?
And to believe me?

See this precious little one,
exposed on my knees,
as on an altar.
I have placed him on a white swaddling cloth,
as on a corporal.
And I am offering him to you
like a holy sacrifice.

This is the child
I brought into the world for you,
for your own good.
So,
when he grows up,
you will not hurt him…

Will you?

In truth,
you are not worthy to receive
this little Lamb of God,
of course.
But,
things being as they are,
you have no reason to hurt Him:
we only hurt people we are afraid of.
You have no reason to be afraid of Him.
He is gentle and humble of heart,

and He only wants
what is best for you.

Contemplate him:
he is defenseless,
he carries no weapon,
he does not know how to fight,
he has no guards,
he has neither a police force, nor an army.
The least among you could slap him,
spit in his face,
and whip him,
without taking the slightest risk
of being punished for it.

Would you want to hurt him
in order to rob him?
What could you take from him—
he does not have two nickels to rub together!
He will not even have a stone on which
to lay his head.
And all that he will have,
the goods that bear fruit
in eternal life,
he will gladly give you,
without measure!

So, you see,
you will not,
ever,
have even the slightest reason to hurt him.

So, we have agreed,
you will not hurt him.

Will you?

He has only come into the world to do good.
Do you want to succeed in life?
Do you want to be happy?
Truly happy?
Invincibly happy?
Then it is simple:
listen to him
and do whatever he tells you.

But I can see what is eating away
at your heart,
I see it well:
it is not enough for you to be happy men,
happy women.
Happy men who make other people happy,
according to their own vocation.
Happy women who make other people happy,
according to their own vocation.
Because, at heart, you dream
of being more than men,
you dream of being more than women.
You are consumed by the desire to be more
than what you are,
so much so that you lose sight
of what you are called to be,
which, however, is more,
infinitely more,
than what Satan makes you want to be.

You would not even be satisfied
by all the world's pleasures
and all the world's delights,
and all the world's ecstasies.
You would not yet be satisfied
by all the world's power,
and all the world's wealth.
You would still not be satisfied

by all the world's renown,
and all the world's adulation,
and all the world's success,
and all the world's glory.

You are and will be perpetually
dissatisfied,
never the heart at peace.

For what you want,
really,
is not to be happy men and women,
nor even blessed.
What devours your heart
is to be like gods,
is to be like gods created by yourselves,
in your image and in your likeness.
Happy gods, if possible.
But, if necessary, in order to be gods,
you are more than willing
to be unhappy gods.
You are more than willing
to make yourselves unhappy
and make other people unhappy,
if it is the price to pay to be like gods.

And yet,
from the foundation of the world,
you should know:
we can no longer be happy
since, in order to be like gods,
we have appropriated the definition
of good and evil for ourselves.

How could you be happy,
since, in order to be like gods,
you no longer want to receive,
from God,
the grace of your happiness?

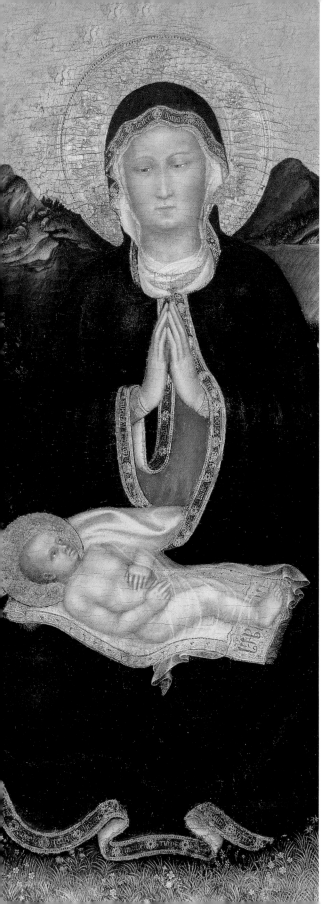

And even then, if you would only be converted
when you came
to the end of your illusions!

Even that is not the case;
you lose your life, going from pleasures
to entertainments,
which please you less and less,
and do not even entertain you…

I ask you,
what is the use of distracting yourself
poorly
from your life here below,
if you are truly destined
for eternal life?

Look at my child
who I am offering to you
like a sacrifice
here,
on my lap:
He alone has the power
to make you blessed,
to reconcile you with God,
to make you succeed in life,
eternally.

In him alone is given to you the grace
of becoming sons of the Most High,
children of God,
heirs forever
to a happiness without end.

So listen to him.
And do whatever he tells you.

But above all,
I beseech you,
do not hurt him!

SILENT CONTEMPLATION

 3 to 5 minutes

Set a timer for the chosen period so that the quality of silence
is not affected by concerns about the time.

*The Heavenly
and Earthly Trinities*
Bartolomé Esteban Murillo
(c. 1681)

OUR FATHER

Our Father in heaven,
holy be your name,
your kingdom come and your will be done,
on earth as in heaven.
Give us today the kind of bread we need.
Forgive us our debts
just as we have forgiven those who are in debt to us.
Do not bring us to the test
but deliver us from the evil one.

CLOSING PRAYER

God our Father, by the hymns of the angels,
you made known the Incarnation of your Son to us:
give us the clear vision of what we must do
in order to live according to his Gospel,
and the force to accomplish it all the days of our life;
may all our actions find their source in him
and receive their completion from him;
guide us to follow him,
in his hidden life as in his public life,
in his compassion and by his cross,
unto the glory of his blessed Resurrection.
Amen.

"Lord, to whom shall we go?
You have the words of eternal life."

Simon Peter's reply to Jesus (John 6:68)

DAY 4

THE MYSTERY OF COMPASSION

In the Paschal Mystery of the compassion of his Son,
true God and true man,
— and what compassion, unto dying,
and even dying on a cross! —
God accomplished the redemption of the world:
we were slaves of sin and death,
and he has brought us out of darkness
and into his own wonderful light.

In the name of the Father,
and of the Son,
and of the Holy Spirit.
Amen.

( ) Recite the opening prayer - p. 30

MUSICAL PRAYER
OF THE HEART

....

THIRD LESSON OF TENEBRAE
François Couperin

....

THIS PROFOUNDLY MOVING MASTERPIECE was concurrent with the death of Louis XIV (1715). It was sung at the night office on Holy Wednesday.

A heartbreaking lament over the fall of Jerusalem (586 B.C.), it is an exhortation to repentance and compassion. Christians borrowed and transformed this poignant and prophetic chant to accompany Christ's Passion in meditation. Yes, he bore the sins of Jerusalem, and ours as well; he, the Savior, has been handed over to the powers of evil, who profane and destroy him! Abandoned by all, even by God, he is defenseless in the hands of his enemies, who will put him to death after subjecting him to a long agony.

The Hebraic letters that serve as titles for the couplets survive from the original poem, the Lamentations, attributed to Jeremiah. Each verse begins with a different letter in the order of the Hebrew alphabet. In the Latin translation of the Hebrew original, this pattern was naturally lost, but the tradition of beginning the verses with the Hebrew letter was retained.

➤ Please note: The Hebrew letter is sung and ornaments the start of each couplet with a long flourish.

....

 13 minutes | How to pray to music - p. 15 | Track 3

....

Jod.

Manum suam misit hostis ad omnia desiderabilia ejus; (bis)
Enemies have stretched out their hands over all her precious things;

quia vidit gentes ingressas sanctuarium suum,
she has even seen the nations invade her sanctuary,

de quibus praeceperas ne intrarent in ecclesiam tuam.
those whom you forbade to enter your congregation.

Caph.

Omnis populus ejus gemens, et quaerens panem:
All her people groan as they search for bread;

dederunt pretiosa quaeque pro cibo ad refocillandam animam.
they trade their treasures for food to revive their strength.

Vide, Domine, et considera, quoniam facta sum vilis. (bis)
Look, O Lord, and see how worthless I have become.

Lamed.

O vos omnes qui transitis per viam,
Is it nothing to you, all you who pass by?

attendite, et videte si est dolor sicut dolor meus: (bis)
Look and see if there is any sorrow like my sorrow,

/quoniam vindemiavit me,
which was brought upon me,

ut locutus est Dominus in die irae furoris sui. (bis)
which the Lord inflicted on the day of his fierce anger.

Mem.

De excelso misit ignem in ossibus meis et erudivit me :
From on high he sent fire; it went deep into my bones;

expandit rete pedibus meis, convertit me retrorsum ;
he spread a net for my feet; he turned me back;

posuit me desolatam, tota die maerore confectam.
he has left me stunned, faint all day long.

Nun.

Vigilavit jugum iniquitatum mearum :
My transgressions were bound into a yoke;

in manu ejus convolutae sunt, et impositae collo meo :
by his hand they were fastened together; they weigh on my neck,

infirmata est virtus mea : (bis)
sapping my strength;

dedit me Dominus in manu, /de qua non potero surgere (x4).
the Lord handed me over to those whom I cannot withstand.

Jerusalem, Jerusalem, convertere ad Dominum Deum tuum (x6).
Jerusalem, Jerusalem, return to the Lord your God.

(🗣) Pause

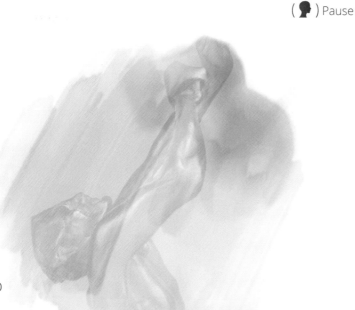

A READING FROM
THE WORD OF GOD

THE LETTER OF SAINT PAUL TO THE COLOSSIANS 1:12-20

 How to read the Word of God - p. 17

[Give] thanks to the Father,
    he has delivered us from the dominion of darkness
    and transferred us to the kingdom of his beloved Son,
    in whom we have redemption, the forgiveness of sins.
He is the image of the invisible God, the first-born of all creation;
    for in him all things were created, in heaven and on earth,
    visible and invisible,
whether thrones or dominions or principalities or authorities—
    all things were created through him and for him.
He is before all things, and in him all things hold together.
    He is the head of the body, the church;
    he is the beginning, the first-born from the dead,
    that in everything he might be pre-eminent.
For in him all the fulness of God was pleased to dwell,
    and through him to reconcile to himself all things,
    whether on earth or in heaven,
    making peace by the blood of his cross.

( ) Pause

MEDITATION

 15 minutes | How to meditate - p. 19

Prayer to be repeated continuously

"Through your death, Lord Jesus, save us from the second death."

MUSICAL PRAYER
OF COMPASSION

....

STABAT MATER

....

THE COMPOSITION OF THE SEQUENCE *STABAT MATER* is attributed to the
great Franciscan poet Jacopone da Todi (1220-1306). It is a moving contemplation on the sorrows endured by Mary of Nazareth as she followed
the Passion and death of her son, Jesus. The *Stabat Mater* has been set to
music by most of the great composers, from Josquin des Prez to Arvo Prät.
The most celebrated version is by Pergolese. The version by Marc-Antoine
Charpentier, which you will now listen to and pray with, is a masterpiece
of classical simplicity. The composer succeeds in ridding it of all that is not
prayer and contemplation. Just at the moment we begin to suspect he has
stripped it down too much, all is revealed.

....

 13 minutes | How to pray to music - p. 15 | Track 4

....

Stabat mater dolorosa juxta crucem lacrimosa dum pendebat Filius.
At the Cross, her station keeping, stood the mournful Mother weeping, close to Jesus to the last.

Cujus animam gementem, contristatam et dolentem, pertransivit gladius.
Through her heart, His sorrow sharing, all His bitter anguish bearing, now at length the sword had passed.

O quam tristis et afflicta fuit illa benedicta Mater Unigeniti.
Oh, how sad and sore distressed was that Mother highly blessed of the sole-begotten One.

Quae moerebat et dolebat, Et tremebat dum videbat Nati poenas incliti.
Christ above in torment hangs, she beneath beholds the pangs of her dying glorious Son.

Quis est homo qui non fleret, Matrem Christi si videret in tanto supplicio?
Is there one who would not weep, whelmed in miseries so deep, Christ's dear Mother to behold?

Quis non posset contristari, piam Matrem contemplari dolentem cum Filio?
Can the human heart refrain from partaking in her pain, in that Mother's pain untold?

Pro peccatis suae gentis vidit Jesum in tormentis et flagellis subditum.
Bruised, derided, cursed, defiled, she beheld her tender Child

Vidit suum dulcem Natum moriendo desolatum, dum emisit spiritum.
For the sins of His own nation, saw Him hang in desolation, till His spirit forth He sent.

Eia, Mater, fons amoris, me sentire vim dolóris, fac, ut tecum lugeam.
O thou Mother! fount of love!, touch my spirit from above, make my heart with thine accord:

Fac, ut ardeat cor meum in amando Christum Deum ut sibi complaceam.
Make me feel as thou hast felt; make my soul to glow and melt with the love of Christ my Lord.

Sancta Mater, istud agas Crucifixi fige plagas Cordi meo valide.
Holy Mother! pierce me through, in my heart each wound renew of my Savior crucified:

Tui Nati vulnerati, tam dignati pro me pati, poenas mecum divide.
Let me share with thee His pain, who for all my sins was slain, who for me in torments died.

Fac, me tecum, pie, flere, Crucifixo condolere, Donec ego vixero.
Let me mingle tears with thee, mourning Him who mourned for me, all the days that I may live:

Juxta crucem tecum stare et me tibi sociare, in planctu desidero.
By the Cross with thee to stay, there with thee to weep and pray, is all I ask of thee to give.

Virgo virginum praeclara, mihi jam non sis amara, fac me tecum plangere.
Virgin of all virgins blest!, Listen to my fond request: let me share thy grief divine;

Fac ut portem Christi mortem, passionis fac consórtem, et plagas recolere.
Let me, to my latest breath, in my body bear the death of that dying Son of thine.

Fac me plagis vulnerari Cruce hac inebriari, et cruore Filii.
Wounded with His every wound, steep my soul till it hath swooned, in His very Blood away;

Flammis ne urar succensus; Per te, virgo, sim defensus, In die judicii.
Be to me, O Virgin, nigh, lest in flames I burn and die, in His awful Judgment Day.

Christe, cum sit hinc exíre, da per Matrem me veníre ad palmam victóriæ.
Christ, when Thou shalt call me hence, by Thy Mother my defense, by Thy Cross my victory;

Quando corpus morietur fac ut animae donetur paradisi gloria. Amen.
While my body here decays, may my soul Thy goodness praise, safe in paradise with Thee.

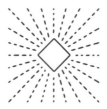

THE MYSTERY

....

ACT IV - THE MYSTERY OF COMPASSION

....

 about 13 minutes

....

Read slowly, respecting the rhythm indicated by the typographic layout.
Pause for a few seconds, where you see ∽.

....

Mary, seated alone, as in a pietà.

THE VIRGIN MARY
Do you remember
when I entrusted him to you,
—My little one, my Child, my love—
I told you,
on behalf of God, his Father,
of God, Our Father:
I told you:
"I brought him into the world for you alone.
Here is my child, my one and only:
I am offering him to you
as a defenseless lamb.
So, please, I beg you:
do not hurt him!

I am giving him to you, but
I beseech you:
do not hurt him…"

Do you remember,
it was on Christmas day.
I had given him to you as a gift,
the most beautiful gift in the world!
There was never
a more beautiful Christmas present.
There will never be a more beautiful
 Christmas present.

A Christmas present for all eternity!
And I simply told you:
"Do not hurt him."

And look!
Look at the state you have put him in!
Look at what you have done to him!
Look at what you have done with him!

He who was gentle and humble in heart,
you have assaulted!
He who came to lift up the trampled reed,
you have crushed!
He who came to revive the flickering wick,
you have extinguished!

My Child, my love:
what have you done to him?

He for whom all things were made,
—and it was very true!—
you have slandered.
He through whom all things were made,
—and it was very beautiful!—
you have disfigured.
He in whom all things were made,
—and it was very good!—
you have hurt in every possible way!

My child, my love:
O my son, my tender lily,
what have you done to him?

He who is your God,
you have accused of blaspheming!
He who came to give you Life,
you have put to death!

You who were created in him;
you who were adopted in him;
you who are, in him, God's own heirs:
what have you done with him?

The Prince of Peace
you have assailed with blows.
The most beautiful of the sons of men
you have despised and rejected.
To the object of divine love,
you have spared no infamy.
The Desire of the Eternal Hills
you have entombed
under the mountain of your filth.

But what has he ever done to you?

Yes, I ask you:
look in the most profound depths
of your conscience,
and answer me:
What has he ever done to you?

For you to lynch him like this,
what could he have done to you?
What possessed you to strike out at him,
like this,
to death?

What has he ever done to you?
Why don't you answer?
Have you nothing to say?

Or rather, are you afraid to say it?

Well, let me tell you
what he has done, and done well, to you.
What he has done to you,
let me tell you frankly,
to your face:
what he has done to you…
is that he has saved you.

Yes, he has really and truly saved you.
He has saved you from death
—and from more than death—
—and from worse than death—
he has saved you from what you deserved:
he has saved you from an eternal life
under the power of Satan.

SILENT CONTEMPLATION

 3 to 5 minutes

Set a timer for the chosen period so that the quality of silence
is not affected by concerns about the time.

Pietà
Daniele Crespi
(1598-1630)

OUR FATHER

Our Father in heaven,
holy be your name,
your kingdom come and your will be done,
on earth as in heaven.
Give us today the kind of bread we need.
Forgive us our debts
just as we have forgiven those who are in debt to us.
Do not bring us to the test
but deliver us from the evil one.

CLOSING PRAYER

Father, you who are infinitely good,
and who wondrously created us
for your beloved Son and in him,
and even more wondrously,
you who have given us a new birth into the divine life
through him, with him, and in him:
crown the triumph of your creating plan
by making us come to share fully in the divinity
of he who humbled himself to share in our humanity
in order to give his life for us on the cross.
Amen.

"It is completed"

Last words of Jesus before his death (John 19:30)

DAY 5

THE TRIUMPH
OF THE HUMAN BODY

When we take and eat
the consecrated host,
the glorious Body of Jesus Christ
returns to himself,
in us,
in order to restore us to our divine purpose.

In the name of the Father,
and of the Son,
and of the Holy Spirit.
Amen.

( ) Recite the opening prayer - p. 30

MUSICAL PRAYER
OF THE HEART

EXSULTET

ON THE NIGHT OF THE FEAST OF EASTER, a bonfire is lit and blessed in front of the church, a fire from which the celebrant lights the Paschal candle. It will be borne in procession into the church, where total darkness gradually gives way to the light of all the candles of the faithful. It is after this procession that the lovely chant of the *Exsultet* rings out. In memory of the heroic crossing of the Red Sea by the Hebrews, it proclaims the eruption of light from the shadows, the Resurrection of Christ, the fulfilment of the Scriptures, and the coming of the end times. The text of the *Exsultet*, in the form of a preface, dates back to Carolingian sacramentaries.

 9 minutes | How to pray to music - p. 15 | ② Track 5

Exsultet jam angelica turba caelorum:
Exult, let them exult, the hosts of heaven,

exsultent divina mysteria:
exult, let Angel ministers of God exult,

et pro tanti Regis victoria tuba insonet salutaris.
let the trumpet of salvation sound aloud our mighty King's triumph!

Gaudeat et tellus tantis irradiata fulgoribus:
Be glad, let earth be glad, as glory floods her,

et aeterni Regis splendore illustrata,
ablaze with light from her eternal King,

totius orbis se sentiat amisisse caliginem.
let all corners of the earth be glad, knowing an end to gloom and darkness.

Laetetur et mater Ecclesia,
Rejoice, let Mother Church also rejoice,

tanti luminis adornata fulgoribus:
arrayed with the lightning of his glory,

et magnis populorum vocibus haec aula resultet.
let this holy building shake with joy, filled with the mighty voices of the peoples.

℣. *Dominus vobiscum.*
The Lord be with you.

℞. *Et cum spiritu tuo.*
And with your spirit.

℣. *Sursum corda.*
Lift up your hearts.

℞. *Habemus ad Dominum.*
We lift them up to the Lord.

℣. *Gratias agamus Domino Deo nostro.*
Let us give thanks to the Lord our God.

℞. *Dignum et justum est.*
It is right and just.

Vere dignum et justum est,
It is truly right and just,

invisibilem Deum Patrem omnipotentem
to acclaim our God invisible, the almighty Father,

Filiumque ejus unigenitum,
and his Only Begotten Son,

Dominum nostrum Jesum Christum,
our Lord Jesus Christ,

toto cordis ac mentis affectu et vocis ministerio personare.
with ardent love of mind and heart and with devoted service of our voice.

Qui pro nobis aeterno Patri Adae debitum solvit,
Who for our sake paid Adam's debt to the eternal Father,

et veteris piaculi cautionem pio cruore detersit.
and, pouring out his own dear Blood, wiped clean the record of our ancient sinfulness.

Haec sunt enim festa paschalia,
These, then, are the feasts of Passover,

in quibus verus ille Agnus occiditur,
in which is slain the Lamb, the one true Lamb,

cujus sanguine postes fidelium consecrantur.
whose Blood anoints the doorposts of believers.

Haec nox est,
This is the night,

in qua primum patres nostros,
when once you led our forebears,

filios Israel eductos de Aegypto,
Israel's children, from slavery in Egypt

Mare Rubrum sicco vestigio transire fecisti.
and made them pass dry-shod through the Red Sea.

Haec igitur nox est,
This is the night

quae peccatorum tenebras, columnae illuminatione purgavit.
that with a pillar of fire banished the darkness of sin.

Haec nox est,
This is the night

quae hodie per universum mundum, in Christo credentes
that even now, throughout the world, sets Christian believers

a vitiis saeculi, et caligine peccatorum segregatos,
apart from worldly vices and from the gloom of sin,

reddit gratiae, sociat sanctitati.
leading them to grace and joining them to his holy ones.

Haec nox est,
This is the night

in qua destructis vinculis mortis,
when Christ broke the prison-bars of death

Christus ab inferis victor ascendit.
and rose victorious from the underworld.

O mira circa nos tuae pietatis dignatio!
O wonder of your humble care for us!

O inaestimabilis dilectio caritatis:
O love, O charity beyond all telling,

ut servum redimeres, Filium tradidisti!
to ransom a slave you gave away your Son!

O certe necessarium Adae peccatum,
O truly necessary sin of Adam,

quod Christi morte deletum est!
destroyed completely by the Death of Christ!

O felix culpa,
O happy fault

quae talem ac tantum meruit habere Redemptorem!
that earned so great, so glorious a Redeemer!

Hujus igitur sanctificatio noctis fugat scelera, culpas lavat,
The sanctifying power of this night dispels wickedness, washes faults away,

et reddit innocentiam lapsis et maestis laetitiam.
restores innocence to the fallen, and joy to mourners.

O vere beata nox,
O truly blessed night,

in qua terrenis caelestia, humanis divina junguntur!
when things of heaven are wed to those of earth, and divine to the human.

In hujus igitur noctis gratia,
On this, your night of grace,

suscipe, sancte Pater, laudis hujus sacrificium vespertinum:
O holy Father, accept this evening sacrifice of praise,

quod tibi in hac cerei oblatione solemni,
this candle, a solemn offering,

per ministrorum manus, de operibus apum, sacrosancta reddit Ecclesia.
the work of bees and of your servants' hands, from your most holy Church.

Oramus ergo te, Domine:
Therefore, O Lord, we pray you

ut cereus iste in honorem tui nominis consecratus,
that this candle, hallowed to the honor of your name,

ad noctis hujus caliginem destruendam, indeficiens perseveret.
may persevere undimmed, to overcome the darkness of this night.

Et in odorem suavitatis acceptus,
Receive it as a pleasing fragrance,

supernis luminaribus misceatur.
and let it mingle with the lights of heaven.

Flammas ejus lucifer matutinus inveniat:
May this flame be found still burning by the Morning Star:

Ille, inquam, lucifer, qui nescit occasum:
the one Morning Star who never sets,

Christus Filius tuus, qui regressus ab inferis,
Christ your Son, who, coming back from death's domain,

humano generi serenus illuxit.
has shed his peaceful light on humanity,

et tecum vivit et regnat, in omnia saecula saeculorum.
and lives and reigns for ever and ever.

℞. *Amen.*
Amen.

( ) Pause

A READING FROM
THE WORD OF GOD

THE GOSPEL ACCORDING TO SAINT LUKE 24:25-34a

 How to read the Word of God - p. 17

He said to them, "O foolish men,
  and slow of heart to believe all that the prophets have spoken!
Was it not necessary that the Christ should suffer these things
  and enter into his glory?"
And beginning with Moses and all the prophets,
  he interpreted to them in all the scriptures the things concerning himself.
  So they drew near to the village to which they were going.
  He appeared to be going further,
but they constrained him, saying,
  "Stay with us, for it is toward evening and the day is now far spent."
So he went in to stay with them.
  When he was at table with them, he took the bread
  and blessed, and broke it, and gave it to them.
And their eyes were opened and they recognized him;
  and he vanished out of their sight.
They said to each other,
  "Did not our hearts burn within us while he talked to us on the road,
  while he opened to us the scriptures?"
And they rose that same hour and returned to Jerusalem;
  and they found the eleven gathered together and those who were with them,
who said, "The Lord has risen indeed!"

 Pause

MEDITATION

 15 minutes | How to meditate - p. 19

Prayer to be repeated continuously

"Blessed are you, Jesus, in your Body given up for us!"

MUSICAL PRAYER
OF HOPE

AVE VERUM CORPUS
Wolfgang Amadeus Mozart

THE TEXT OF THE *AVE VERUM CORPUS* is a 14th-century hymn attributed to Pope Innocent VI. It was sung during the Mass, at the elevation of the host, after the consecration. Beginning in the Renaissance, many great composers set it to music. In 1791, knowing he was dying, Mozart was with his wife, who was expecting their sixth child. He composed this marvelous music as he was reflecting on the holy Viaticum (the communion of the dying) he would soon receive, and which constitutes, as stated in the last verse, a foretaste of the glorious Body of Christ we will rejoin the moment we cross the threshold of death.

 4 minutes | How to pray to music - p. 15 | Track 6

Ave, verum corpus natum de Maria Virgine;
Hail, true Body, born of the Virgin Mary,

Vere passum, immolatum in Cruce pro homine:
Having truly suffered, sacrificed on the cross for mankind,

Cujus latus perforatum unda fluxit et sanguine
You from whose pierced side water and blood flowed:

Esto nobis praegustatum mortis in examine.
In the trial of death, be for us the foretaste of yourself.

THE MYSTERY

ACT V - THE TRIUMPH OF THE HUMAN BODY

 about 7 minutes

Read slowly, respecting the rhythm indicated by the typographic layout.
Pause for a few seconds, where you see ∿.

Mary Magdalene and Jesus, near the tomb,
on Easter morning.

MARY MAGDALENE
Hail,
watchman!
How dark is the night?

JESUS
The darkness has been overcome.
Behold, over Zion,
a radiant dawn
is rising.

MARY MAGDALENE
You, there, come closer!
Tell me,
where have you laid
the body of my Lord?
Tell me where you have put him,
so that I may go to prepare his body for
burial.

JESUS
Mary!

MARY MAGDALENE
Rabbouni!

JESUS
Mary, O Mary,
do not touch me,
do not hold me here!
I must leave.

MARY MAGDALENE
How?
After all we have been through…
I have found you
alive!
And now you must leave me
right away?

JESUS
O Mary,
do not seek to keep me here.
I am no longer of this world.
I must return to the house of my Father,
your Father and your God.

MARY MAGDALENE
Lord,
you who know everything,
you must know this well:
Each time they gave you a blow,
I received it also;
Each time they drove a nail into your hands
and your feet,

it was in my hands
and my feet they drove it, as well.

O my Jesus!
Each time your flesh suffered a wound,
I prayed it had been inflicted upon me,
rather than upon you!
I would have suffered so much less!

And your final cry,
it was heartrending!
And the thrust of the lance
right in the middle of your heart!
They also pierced this heart,
which loves you so!

Lord,
behold, I have found you
wondrously alive!
And you would stop me from throwing
myself at your feet,
and washing them, again and again,
with all the tears in my body?

JESUS
Mary, O Mary,
in Simon's house,
with the flood of your tears of penitence,
and the perfume of your love,
you washed
my living body.

At the foot of the Cross,
with your tears of grief,
you prepared
my dead body for burial.

And behold, now,
with your tears of joy,

you have just anointed
my glorious body.

Blessed are you, Mary,
for your fair love:
it has gained you the privilege
of inaugurating with me
the new day rising over the world.

Blessed are you, Mary,
my little sheep who was lost.
How beautiful have you again become,
through your faith and your love!

MARY MAGDALENE
O Lord,
all those men
only saw my body,
my feminine body,
as something to be taken or to be despised,
as something to be possessed or to be stoned.
Among men,
you alone saw who I am,
you alone knew who I was.
You have made me beautiful in my own eyes.

JESUS
Yes, you are beautiful, O Mary:
your heart has known to show more love
than all the sins your existence could bear.

MARY MAGDALENE
Oh, Lord!
Who will free me from this body of misery!
This body subject to the ravages of time,
this body made to suffer and to die.
This body marked by my sins.

JESUS
Just because you once let concupiscence
take over your heart,
do not now
despise your body!

Even fallen because of sin,
your body,
your human body,
remains a wonder,
the masterpiece of your Creator.

Yes, I bless you,
Father, God of heaven and of earth:
to crown all your creation,
you desired to mold the human body
in me and for me.

Thus,
according to your benevolent plan,
you created the human being,
man and woman,
predestined in love to form but one flesh,
icon of the eternal wedding banquet
of your only begotten Son
with created humanity.

I give you thanks, Father,
for consecrating your Creation to me
through this great mystery,
and for sending me
to incarnate it in human history
so that, despite the jealousy of the rebel
angels
and the Fall of humanity,
it would be accomplished for all eternity.

Thank you, Father,
for this human body,

which you have made the form
of your beloved Son.

Thank you, Father,
for this human body,
conceived of the Holy Spirit
and born of the Virgin Mary.

Thank you, Father,
for this human body,
which the shepherds and kings
once adored!

Thank you, Father,
for this human body
whose tongue is your Word.

Thank you, Father,
for this human body,
which was given up to death;
and thank you for its precious blood,
which was spilled
for your glory
and for the salvation of the world.

Thank you, Father,
for my body in its agony,
whose sweat became blood.

Thank you, Father,
for my outraged body,
crowned with thorns.

Thank you, Father,
for my exhausted body,
three times fallen,
crushed
under the weight of the sins of the world.

Thank you, Father,
for my body,
whose hands and feet were pierced by nails.

Thank you, Father,
for my body with outstretched arms
drawing a cross over the world.

Thank you, Father,
for my moribund body,
commending its final breath into your
hands.

Thank you, Father,
for my body
whose heart was pierced by the lance.

Thank you, Father,
for this human body
through which your will was done,
perfectly,
unto the end.

Thank you, Father,
for my body, which you lifted up,
free
and in triumph.

Thank you, Father,
for this human body,
now glorious,
sin's conqueror,
in which you have made
all your Creation
victorious.

Thank you, Father,
for this resurrected body,
in which you are returning all of humankind

to your grace,
and opening the Communion of the Saints
to them.

And now, O most loving Father,
as a supreme testimony of your tenderness,
welcome this human body into your breast,
so that all may be perfectly accomplished
according to the sublime design of your love.

MARY MAGDALENE
Lord, what you have just said…
your prayer to your Father,
to our Father, to our God…
you have the words of eternal Life!

JESUS
Mary, O Mary,
no, no, do not cry,
do not cry.
Rather,
rejoice!
All the hope I came
to make rise up in you
will be fulfilled!

You also
will be raised from the dead
in your body!

You will all become, forever, glorious bodies,
I incorporated in you,
and you incorporated in me!

And you will come to join me there,
in my dwelling place,
your dwelling place,
in God.

MARY MAGDALENE
O Lord,
may everything be done
according to your word.

But make it so that,
for me,
it happens right away!

JESUS
No disciple is above his Master:
to join me there where I am going,
you must also,
following after me, in my name,
in my person,
make your bodies,
your blood,
your lives,
a living offering of love
unto the end,
until you cross over, victoriously,
through the baptism of death.

But, I promise you,
along this earthly pilgrimage
you still have to accomplish,
you will never be alone!
I am with you until the end of time.

MARY MAGDALENE
How can you leave us,
even as you stay with us?
How can such a thing come about?

JESUS
Remember what I told you
during my last Passover meal:

"Do this in memory of me."

Truly, truly,
when you come together in my Name
around a meal;
when,
in memory of me,
you will break the bread,
bless it,
share it and eat it,
I will be there,
really,
substantially
present at the heart of your lives.
By your communion
in my Body given up for you,
I will be in you,
as you
will be in me.

Yes, I say to you:
when,
in memory of me,
you will take and eat
the consecrated bread,
it will be my Body
coming back to itself
in you,
to restore you to your
divine vocation.

And thus,
when you go towards others
to serve them and to love them,
it will be as what you are,
in reality and in truth:
the acting members
of my Eucharistic body.

So,
by your lives given
in communion with my life
in you,
it is I who will come to all
in all.
It is I who will come to you.

O my disciples, my friends,
how beautiful is the will of our Father:
you are consecrated to be
my Body acting in the world,
my real presence in the world,
until I come again!

And you, woman,
behold, I am choosing you
and I am sending you out
to be the apostle of my Apostles.

Go to find my disciples
and say to them:
"The Lord lives,
truly, he is risen!
And I have seen His glorious body!
Alleluia!"

SILENT CONTEMPLATION

 3 to 5 minutes

Set a timer for the chosen period so that the quality of silence
is not affected by concerns about the time.

Noli me tangere
Antonio Raggi
(1624-1686)

OUR FATHER

Our Father in heaven,
holy be your name,
your kingdom come and your will be done,
on earth as in heaven.
Give us today the kind of bread we need.
Forgive us our debts
just as we have forgiven those who are in debt to us.
Do not bring us to the test
but deliver us from the evil one.

CLOSING PRAYER

Lord Jesus Christ,
you made the glory of your Resurrection shine forth in splendor over all creation
and you have gone to prepare a place for us,
at the right hand of God, your Father and ours;
and yet you do not abandon us,
for you leave us a foretaste of our eternal communion in your divinity
when we celebrate the memorial of your saving Passion:
give us to receive, from a love so great,
the mysteries of your Body, given up for us,
so that we may harvest, even in this present time, the fruits of our redemption.
You who are God, with the Father and the Holy Spirit.
Amen.

"As you, Father,
are in me, and I in you,
that they also may be in us,
I in them and you in me."

Prayer of Jesus to his Father and ours (cf. John 17:21-23)

DAY 6

THE TRIUMPH
OF THE NEW COMMANDMENT

In our existence each day,

during our entire earthly pilgrimage,

here's how we may bring the benevolent plan of the Father to fruition,

against all odds:

by loving one another as Jesus has loved us.

So, our eternal life has begun already:

what we do to our neighbor, we do to God,

what our neighbor does to us, he does to God.

Thus, we already love and are loved

as God loves and God is loved in the Kingdom of heaven.

In the name of the Father,
and of the Son,
and of the Holy Spirit.
Amen.

( ) Recite the opening prayer - p. 30

MUSICAL PRAYER OF THE HEART

ABIDE WITH ME
Henry Francis Lyte

ABIDE WITH ME IS A HYMN WRITTEN IN 1847 by Henry Francis Lyte. Seriously ill with tuberculosis, he wrote this heartrending prayer on his death-bed. He survived its composition by only three weeks. *Abide with Me* is here sung to the music of *Eventide*, composed in 1861 by William Henry Monk.

 4 minutes | How to pray to music - p. 15 | (2) Track 7

Abide with me; fast falls the eventide;

The darkness deepens; Lord, with me abide!

When other helpers fail and comforts flee,

Help of the helpless, O abide with me.

Swift to its close ebbs out life's little day;

Earth's joys grow dim, its glories pass away;

Change and decay in all around I see;

O Thou who changest not, abide with me.

I need Thy presence every passing hour;

What but Thy grace can foil the tempter's power?

Who, like Thyself, my guide and stay can be?

Through cloud and sunshine, Lord, abide with me.

I fear no foe, with Thee at hand to bless;

Ills have no weight, and tears no bitterness;

Where is death's sting? Where, grave, thy victory?

I triumph still, if Thou abide with me.

Hold Thou Thy cross before my closing eyes;

Shine through the gloom and point me to the skies;

Heaven's morning breaks, and earth's vain shadows flee;

In life, in death, O Lord, abide with me.

 Pause

141

A READING FROM
THE WORD OF GOD

FIRST LETTER OF SAINT JOHN 3:1a, 10-11, 13, 16, 18, 22-23; 4:7-12

 How to read the Word of God - p. 17

See what love the Father has given us,
    that we should be called children of God;
and so we are.
By this it may be seen who are the children of God,
    and who are the children of the devil:
    whoever does not do right is not of God,
    nor he who does not love his brother.
For this is the message which you have heard from the beginning,
    that we should love one another.

By this we know love,
    that he laid down his life for us;
    and we ought to lay down our lives for the brethren.

Little children, let us not love in word or speech but in deed and in truth.

We receive from him whatever we ask,
    because we keep his commandments
    and do what pleases him.
And this is his commandment,
    that we should believe in the name of his Son Jesus Christ
    and love one another,
    just as he has commanded us.

Beloved, let us love one another; for love is of God,
 and he who loves is born of God and knows God.
He who does not love does not know God; for God is love.
In this the love of God was made manifest among us,
that God sent his only Son into the world, so that we might live through him.
In this is love,
 not that we loved God
 but that he loved us and sent his Son
 to be the expiation for our sins.
Beloved, if God so loved us,
 we also ought to love one another.
No man has ever seen God;
 if we love one another, God abides in us
 and his love is perfected in us.

( ) Pause

MEDITATION

 15 minutes | How to meditate - p. 19

Prayer to be repeated continuously

"Jesus, our brother,
teach us to love you
as you want to be loved!"

MUSICAL PRAYER
OF HOPE

UBI CARITAS

THIS ANTIPHON WOULD SEEM TO DATE BACK TO THE 8TH CENTURY, when it first appeared in the Monastery of Saint-Gall, in Switzerland. It is one of the antiphons sung during the washing of the feet at the Mass of the Lord's Supper, on Holy Thursday. When Jesus had washed his disciples' feet and taken his place back at the table, he said to them, "Do you know what I have done to you?" and then he added, "I have given you an example, that you also should do as I have done to you. If you know these things, blessed are you if you do them!" (see Jn 13:12-17). The antiphon masterfully sums up this teaching of Christ, which constitutes the essential clause of his Testament: communion in his Body and in his Blood is absolutely inseparable from the new commandment, and vice versa. In this regard, in some very ancient manuscripts and since 1969 in the Roman Missal, the text of the refrain is: *Ubi caritas est vera, Deus est*, which means, "Where love is true, God is present." "As I have done for you... As I have loved you": this is true Love.

 3 minutes | How to pray to music - p. 15 | Track 8

Ubi caritas et amor, Deus ibi est.
Where true charity is dwelling, God is present there.

Congregavit nos in unum Christi amor.
By the love of Christ we have been brought together:

Exsultemus, et in ipso jucundemur.
let us find in him our gladness and our pleasure;

Timeamus, et amemus Deum vivum.
may we love him and revere him, God the living,

Et ex corde diligamus nos sincero.
and in love respect each other with sincere hearts.

Ubi caritas et amor, Deus ibi est.
Where true charity is dwelling, God is present there.

Simul ergo cum in unum congregamur:
So when we as one are gathered all together,

Ne nos mente dividamur, caveamus.
let us strive to keep our minds free of division;

Cessent jurgia maligna, cessent lites.
may there be an end to malice, strife and quarrels,

Et in medio nostri sit Christus Deus.
and let Christ our God be dwelling here among us.

Ubi caritas et amor, Deus ibi est.
Where true charity is dwelling, God is present there.

Simul quoque cum beatis videamus,
May your face thus be our vision, bright in glory,

Glorianter vultum tuum, Christe Deus:
Christ our God, with all the blessed Saints in heaven:

Gaudium quod est immensum, atque probum,
such delight is pure and faultless, joy unbounded,

Saecula per infinita saeculorum. Amen.
which endures through countless ages, world without end. Amen.

THE MYSTERY

 about 7 minutes

Read slowly, respecting the rhythm indicated by the typographic layout.
Pause for a few seconds, where you see ∼.

Jesus appears to Saint Paul.

SAINT PAUL
Paul is my name.

I was once called Saul.

Yes, I was that persecutor,
that blasphemer,
that slanderer;
threats and slaughter, the air I breathed.

At the merest mention
of the name of Jesus, the Christ,
I shook with rage.

Then, as I made my way to Damascus,
the one I was persecuting,
Jesus himself,
threw me off my mount.
And behold,
blinding me with his light,
he revealed his glory to me.

Thus,
teaching me at length,
directly,
he bestowed
knowledge of the mysteries upon me.

At last,
he called me to his service,
and deigned to choose me,
as one untimely born,
so that henceforth
my weakness
could manifest his power.

Thus,
the Lord Jesus
accorded me the grace of being his Apostle,
herald of the Gospel of God,
pillar of his Church,
—with Peter—
so that sanctified in the Holy Spirit
the pagans would become
a most sweet offering
to the heavenly Father.

But…
This light…
Could it be…
Lord, is it you?
Behold, you have come back to visit me!

JESUS
Yes, Paul,
it is indeed I!

Good and faithful servant,
worthy to enter into the joy of his master,
you are fighting the good fight.
And soon,
you will receive the crown of victory.

However,
your race is not yet finished…
So that you may fight it
to the end,
I must still put the finishing touches
on your instruction.
I must still initiate you into
the ultimate mystery of salvation,
the same one I revealed
to my disciples,
my friends,
on the eve of my death,
after the Traitor went out
into the night.

SAINT PAUL
Speak, Lord,
your servant is listening.

JESUS
Truly, truly,
I say to you:
In order to be holy and blameless
before God,
it is not necessary
for you,
certainly not,
to seek perfection
through some spiritual path,
however beneficial it might be.

SAINT PAUL
What must be done,
then,
to attain holiness?

JESUS
God alone is Holy!
You must,
therefore,
let divine Love attain
its perfection
in you.

SAINT PAUL
But Lord, that is impossible!
How can such a thing come about?

JESUS
For this purpose,
there is just one, single, simple
path,
the simplest there could be:
It is enough to love…

SAINT PAUL
It is enough to love…
Lord, see that
as a faithful observer of the Law,
I have practiced this Great Commandment
from my youth:
"To love God with all my heart,
with all my soul and with all my mind
and to love my neighbor as myself…"

JESUS
Be on your guard!
Like you,

the scribes and the Pharisees,
the Doctors of the Law and the high priests,
like you, they also
loved God with all their heart,
with all their soul, and with all their mind.

But when the true and living God
came to visit them,
when God
in person
made himself their neighbor,
not only did they not recognize him,
they even convicted him of blasphemy,
they visited outrages upon him,
they condemned him to death,
and even to death on a cross.

They loved God with all their heart,
they loved God with all their soul,
and they loved God with all their mind!

And me?

They did not love me…

Paul,
no one knows this better than you do:
the Law and the Prophets were given to them
so that, when I came,
they would recognize my voice,
they would listen to me,
and they would love me…

And so I am sending you,
you, Saul become Paul,
through grace;
behold, I am sending you to your brothers,
my brothers,

and you will tell them this:
"I, Paul, the Lord's Apostle,
am going to show you the path that
surpasses
all other paths:
Love one another
as Jesus Christ has loved us!"

On this Earth,
there is no other way
of being certain of loving God
as he has desired to give himself
for being loved.

There is no other rule of life
for whomever desires to be judged worthy
of entering, already in this present time,
into the Communion of the Saints
and dwelling there forever.

SAINT PAUL
The Law of Moses commands
that we love our neighbor as ourselves;
is this not
already
the same as your new commandment?

JESUS
Truly, truly,
I say to you:
You must love your neighbor
not as yourself,
but more than yourself:
you must love others as God,
in person,
in my person,
has loved you.

There is no other way to be saved
and to save the world!

O, how hardheaded you must be,
to refuse to hear this!

Even the best,
the disciples I chose for myself,
whom I set aside,
whom I taught personally,
openly,
on the mountain,
or in the boat;
my friends for whom I prayed to the Father,
and pleaded for,
on my knees in the desert,
from twilight until dawn;
even the three who saw me,
really and truly, saw me
transfigured,
even they
refused to hear
my new commandment!

Ah! Even they,
just like you,
tried the best they could to love God
with all their hearts
and their neighbor as themselves!
But, when the time came to follow me
to the end,
to love their neighbor,
not as themselves,
but as more than themselves,
even unto giving their own lives for him,
then and there, they turned away.

When the time came to love unto the end,
when the time came to give

the greatest proof of love:
when the time came to give their lives
for those they love,
then they fled,
into the night…

Now,
behold,
the Holy Spirit is guiding you to the truth
in its fullness:
Then,
you will understand what it is to love.
And the Spirit will instill
in you
the desire to love others as God loves them,
and to love God
as God desires to be loved.

And then,
in communion with the Spirit of God,
you will give your life
so that in you,
the Love of God may reach its perfection.

Saint Paul
If that is the case,
then the new and eternal Law
abolishes the Commandments
of the Law of Moses.

Jesus
The first commandment of the Law of Moses,
and the second, which is like it,
I have neither abolished, nor changed:
I have accomplished them
in an overflowing fullness,
in an infinite overabundance,
since in me,
loving God and loving one's brother,

loving God and loving one's neighbor,
has, in truth,
become the same thing.

Just as well,
in the new and eternal Covenant
there is only one, unique commandment left,
my new commandment,
the one I left you as a testament
on the eve of my death:
"Love one another as I have loved you."

If you keep this inheritance,
my inheritance;
if you make it increase
in your lives:
then, I promise you,
the world will recognize you as my friends.
And soon, following you,
—What am I saying?—
Following your example!
They will be countless,
those in whom the love of God
will attain its perfection!

"See how they love one another!"
"See how,
in them,
the Lord does great things!"
they will say,
astounded,
converted to the love of God
by seeing you love each other.

Truly, truly,
I say to you:
If you put my new Commandment
into practice,
if,

not with words and with thoughts,
but in deed and in truth,
you are beloved to the end,
loving to the end,
then you will be my love for others
until I come again;
and you will accomplish my work.
I am the one your lives will make manifest;
and the world will recognize me,
and the world will love me.
And thus,
the world will recognize its God,
and the world will love,
in deed and in truth,
the true and living God.

And all, yes, all of you,
—All of us!—
you in me and I in you,
with a single heart, with a single soul,
and a single mind,
we will love the Lord our God,
my Father,
and yours,
in the communion of the Holy Spirit.

And then,
in you,
you in me and I in you,
the Love of God will attain its perfection.

SILENT CONTEMPLATION

 3 to 5 minutes

Set a timer for the chosen period so that the quality of silence
is not affected by concerns about the time.

The Good Samaritan
George Frederic Watts
(1852)

OUR FATHER

Our Father in heaven,
holy be your name,
your kingdom come and your will be done,
on earth as in heaven.
Give us today the kind of bread we need.
Forgive us our debts
just as we have forgiven those who are in debt to us.
Do not bring us to the test
but deliver us from the evil one.

CLOSING PRAYER

God our Father,
you have made us your sons in your beloved Son, Jesus Christ:
allow us to reject what is not worthy of his Name
and to seek only what honors him;
may your Spirit of love come into our hearts
and make us capable of loving one another
as your Son has loved us;
thus do you desire to make us your witnesses
and to form in us, already in this present time,
the love with which we will love you eternally.
Through Jesus Christ, your Son, our Savior, who with you, is Love,
in the communion of the Holy Spirit.
Amen.

"You are my friends
if you do what I command you.
This is my commandment,
that you love one another
as I have loved you."

Jesus' Last Testament (Jn 15:14, 12)

DAY 7
LOVE'S FINAL TRIUMPH

God, our Father, in his Providence,
watches over our earthly pilgrimage,
the prologue to our eternal life,
for he desired for us, already in this present time,
to be saved, and already active members
of the glorious body of his Son, Jesus Christ,
in whom the hope of the blessed Resurrection
has shone forth for the multitude.
He is our brother, he who carried the Cross of all our sins;
he is our advocate, he who continuously
offers himself for our Salvation;
and it is he who will return at the end of time,
to judge, on the basis of our love,
whether we are worthy —or not— to rejoin him
in the bosom of God his Father,
in that place where there will be
no more grief, nor tears, nor suffering,
but only joy and happiness forever,
for in that place, Divine Love will be all in all.

In the name of the Father,
and of the Son,
and of the Holy Spirit.
Amen.

( ) Recite the opening prayer - p. 30

MUSICAL PRAYER
OF THE HEART

....

LIBERA ME
Gabriel Fauré

....

THE *LIBERA ME* IS A HYMN SUNG AT THE END OF THE FUNERAL (or *Requiem*)
Mass, during the final commendation.

Fauré began composing his *Requiem* after the death of his father in 1885
and completed it shortly after the death of his mother on New Year's Eve,
1888. Fauré thus said of his work: "It's been said that my *Requiem* does
not convey the horror of death. But this is my feeling about death: it is
a happy deliverance, a hope of happiness in the hereafter, rather than a
sorrowful crossing over." And, indeed, his *Requiem* introduces a medita-
tive, mysterious, and calming expressiveness through music, conducive
to contemplating the Love of God. For Fauré, the word "God," was, indeed,
"just the monumental synonym for the word Love."

....

 5 minutes | How to pray to music - p.15 | Track 9

....

BARITONE

Libera me, Domine, de morte aeterna,
Deliver me, O Lord, from death eternal

in die illa tremenda, in die illa :
on that fearful day,

*quando caeli movendi sunt (*bis*) et terra.*
when the heavens and the earth shall be moved,

Dum veneris judicare saeculum per ignem.
when thou shalt come to judge the world by fire.

CHOIR *moderato*

Tremens factus sum ego, et timeo,
I am made to tremble, and I fear,

dum discussio venerit, atque ventura ira.
till the judgment be upon us, and the coming wrath.

CHOIR *piu mosso*

Dies illa, dies irae, calamitatis et miseriae,
That day, day of wrath, calamity and misery,

Dies illa, dies magna et amara valde.
day of great and exceeding bitterness!

Requiem aeternam dona eis, Domine,
Eternal happiness grant unto them, O Lord:

et lux perpetua luceat eis, luceat eis.
and let light perpetual shine upon them.

CHOIR *moderato*

Libera me, Domine, de morte aeterna,
Deliver me, O Lord, from death eternal

in die illa tremenda, in die illa,
on that fearful day,

Quando caeli movendi sunt (bis) *et terra.*
when the heavens and the earth shall be moved,

Dum veneris judicare saeculum per ignem.
when thou shalt come to judge the world by fire.

BARITONE

Libera me, Domine, de morte aeterna.
Deliver me, O Lord, from death eternal.

Libera me, Domine…
Deliver me, O Lord.

) Pause

A READING FROM
THE WORD OF GOD

First Letter of Saint John 4:17-20; 5:3a

 How to read the Word of God - p. 17

In this is love perfected with us,
    that we may have confidence for the day of judgment,
    because as he is so are we in this world.
There is no fear in love,
    but perfect love casts out fear.
    For fear has to do with punishment,
    and he who fears is not perfected in love.

We love, because he first loved us.
If any one says, "I love God," and hates his brother, he is a liar;
    for he who does not love his brother whom he has seen,
    cannot love God whom he has not seen.
For this is the love of God, that we keep his commandments.

) Pause

MEDITATION

 15 minutes | How to meditate - p. 19

Prayer to repeat continuously

"Jesus, when you come again, bring us into the joy of the Father."

MUSICAL PRAYER
OF HOPE

IN PARADISUM
Gabriel Fauré

THE *IN PARADISUM* IS A GREGORIAN ANTIPHON sung at the end of the funeral Mass, after the *Libera me*, as the procession forms to accompany the coffin of the deceased from the church to the cemetery.

Rather than a dramatic evocation of the Last Judgment, Fauré here proposes a serene vision full of hope after death, seen in the light of Paradise. However, the mention at the end of the antiphon of the poor man, Lazarus, from the parable, can only cause hardened, prideful hearts to fear the fate of the evil rich man, forever separated from God and the blessed.

 4 minutes | How to pray to music - p. 15 | Track 10

In Paradisum deducant te Angeli,
May the angels lead you into paradise;

in tuo adventu suscipiant te martyres,
may the martyrs receive you at your arrival

et perducant te in civitatem sanctam Jerusalem (x 4).
and lead you to the holy city Jerusalem.

Chorus angelorum te suscipiat,
May choirs of angels receive you,

*et cum Lazaro quondam paupere (*bis*)*
and with Lazarus, once a poor man,

*aeternam habeas requiem! (*bis*)*
may you have eternal happiness!

THE MYSTERY

ACT VII - LOVE'S FINAL TRIUMPH

 about 8 minutes

Read slowly, respecting the rhythm indicated by the typographic layout.
Pause for a few seconds, where indicated ◟.

Controversy between Saint John and Lucifer

SAINT JOHN
…Signed: John. Disciple of Jesus Christ.
There.
I have finished my letter
to the Seven Churches of Asia,
…on the subject of the Last Judgment.

…This question has generated
so much worry and discussion
within their communities…

…Let us read it one more time:
"My beloved:
you know that
Christ, our Lord,
will come again in glory
to judge the living and the dead.

And you also know that
on that day,
we will all be judged based upon Love,
and upon what authentic love,
if not the love we have shown
for one another?

Oh! How I yearn for the coming
of that last day!

Humanity will have drifted
for centuries and centuries
on the tide of history,
through tempests
and shipwrecks.
At last, she will arrive at port,
at grace's harbor.
And there,
the benevolent plan of our Creator,
of our God and Father,
will be accomplished
definitively,
for the best
and…
…it can only be for the best,
since God is Love!

"Beloved,
for us, who await
the return of our Lord
with impatience,
for us,
this last day of time
can only be a blessed day
among all days:
the day when,
in Christ's Parousia, his return,
the truth of Creation
will be made manifest."

Come, Lord Jesus!
Do not be long!

On that day,
everything will become clear.
We will understand everything!
All of us, with all that we are,
will behold and adore
the will of God…
as it has been accomplished!

And we will be able
to give thanks,
eternally,
for the supreme beauty
of our
purpose.

*As Saint John is speaking, Lucifer appears
and discretely approaches from behind.*

O yes!
That day, blessed among days!
When the power of the Resurrection of the Lord
will be made manifest
in the full accomplishment of his Incarnation!

For, behold, in the final instant
on the last day,
through his Only Begotten Son
Jesus Christ,
—one of us!—
God will forever be
all in all.

LUCIFER
Ah, ah, what you have written is so beautiful!

You know, it's so beautiful I could almost
cry!

But you know as well as I do that it is not
true!
You know I have my role to play
so that the worst happens,
and for the worst!

SAINT JOHN

Lucifer!
You! In my own house!
How dare you visit me!
Most vile tempter!

LUCIFER

Do not get yourself all worked up!
I come as a friend.

I saw that you had written a book,
the Apocalypse.
A work that predicts
what will happen at the end of the world,
when God will judge the living and the dead.

So, you see,
I need you to share with me
some of the revelations you have received.
For,
you see,
I also care about readying myself
to accomplish, as best as possible,
God's will.

SAINT JOHN

Foul spirit,
I have no part to play
with you!
Away, Satan!

LUCIFER

Oh, so petulant!
You speak of gentleness
and tenderness
to the entire world,
and look at the way you treat me!

I am not asking you to betray
any of your secrets,
I am just asking you to tell me,
more clearly than the way
in which you wrote it,
how many men and women will be damned.

SAINT JOHN

It is always a mistake to listen
and to converse with you!
I told you: get away!

LUCIFER

You may assume that, since I am here,
speaking with you,
God has given me permission,
just as he gave me his permission to come
to Christ in the desert
at just the right time.

Therefore, you cannot send me away
until you have answered me.
According to your sources,
how many will there be,
ultimately,
in the number of the damned?

SAINT JOHN

That number has not been revealed to me.

LUCIFER

Liar!

You wrote yourself that there would
only be 144,000 among the saved.
Ha, ha!
Make the calculation:
All the men and all the women
of all time,
minus 144,000;
that will make billions upon billions
of clients for me!

SAINT JOHN

I have also written:
"I beheld a great multitude,
which no man could number,
of all nations, and peoples, and tongues.
The Lamb will lead them to sources
of living water,
and God will wipe away all the tears
from their eyes."

LUCIFER

But you also wrote:
"The fearful, the lukewarm, the renegades,
the depraved, the impure, the idolaters,
will have their part in the sea burning
with fire and brimstone:
this is the second death!"
And, in the same vein,
your friend Paul has written:
"Do not be deceived,
neither fornicators, nor adulterers,
nor sodomites, nor thieves, nor profiteers,
nor the covetous, nor the quarrelsome,
nor the violent, nor slanderers,
nor drunkards will enter
into the Kingdom of God."
So you see, it is going to get crowded
down at my place,
where it is nice and warm!

SAINT JOHN

I have also written:
"God is Love."
And my friend Paul has also written:
"Love is long-suffering,
Love bears all things,
Love believes all things,
Love hopes all things,
Love endures all things.
Love does not disappoint."

LUCIFER

Now,
tell me you are not going
to pretend Jesus was deceiving you
when he said:
"Wide and broad is the road
that leads to destruction!"
Well, that should clear up any doubts,
and that is the Gospel truth!

So, to recap,

He counts on his fingers

If my calculations are right,
from the beginning
until the end of the world,
all those who, one time or another,
have neglected to aid their neighbor,
or refused to forgive him,
plus all those who have lived in sin,
and, may I add,
all those who did not have faith,
plus all those who were not baptized:

He rubs his hands together and cackles

That makes billions and billions
of godforsaken people
for whom I am going to have to prepare
a dwelling
of eternal torture!

SAINT JOHN

Jesus also said:
 "The will of my Father
is that not one of the ones he has given me
may be lost."
And again:
"When I will be lifted up from the earth,
I will draw all men to myself."

And did he not say to Peter, in front of me:
"For men,
it is impossible to be saved.
But for God,
all things are possible"?

Therefore, no one can claim to say
how many will be saved,
nor how many will be damned.
That is the secret of the Father.

What I do know,
with absolute certainty,
and you also know it,
with the same absolute certainty,
is this:
At the end of history,
in one way or another,
as God wills it,
the triumph of his Love will be

total,
full,
perfect,
without a shadow.
Not even yours,
fallen angel of light!

LUCIFER

Your words are no more than the lies
of a fanatic!
Amen, I say to you:
At the end of the world,
there will be no faith left on earth.
I will have won!

SAINT JOHN

You
are the Father of Lies!

As for me, I tell the truth.
You know it,
and that is what enrages you:
you do not have the power
to foil
God's plan.

LUCIFER

Liar!
You know nothing of this!

SAINT JOHN

I know very well,
as well as you know it yourself:
all your plans
to harm the human race
will be,
in the end,

most certainly,
and completely,
foiled.

For, as you well know,
if God were All-Powerful,
but not All-Loving,
you could perhaps have hoped to harm
humanity,
at least, in some way,
once and for all.

If God were All-Loving,
but not All-Powerful,
you could perhaps have hoped
to succeed in stealing from him
at least a few victims to devour,
once and for all.

But,
since God is All-Loving
as well as All-Powerful,
you have never been able to hope,
not even for a moment,
from the foundation of the world,
even after having won
decisive battles
against humanity;
even after having tainted the human heart
with the cancer of sin;
even after having brought
evil, suffering, and death
into the heart of every human life;
even after all your victories,
as countless as they have been,
—it is true!—
even after having obtained the humiliation

and the death
of God's Christ
—himself!—
on a Cross;
even at that favorable moment
when your shadows darkened the entire
Cosmos,
even at that instant of your triumph,
the Creator of Heaven and of Earth
never let you hope
a single second,
and that is your eternal torment;
God has never left you
the slightest hope.

And above all, the hope that
he would leave the slightest possibility
in the final accomplishment
of his benevolent plan,
for the slightest definitive success,
even minuscule,
even imperceptible,
of your malevolent plan
for humanity.

You know this well;
you know it very well;
you know it better than anyone.

You understood it
once and for all
when God so loved humanity
that He gave them His own Son
so that they would become
a single flesh
together,
and so that their destinies would be

bound together
forever.

Yes, you know it better than anyone:
at the end of time,
you, Lucifer,
will be left, in the end,
with no possibility of winning anything—
—none whatsoever!
For
these truths cannot be separated:
God is Love,
and with God, nothing is impossible.

SILENT CONTEMPLATION

 3 to 5 minutes

Set a timer for the chosen period so that the quality of silence
is not affected by concerns about the time.

*The Return
of the Prodigal Son*
Rembrandt
(c. 1668)

OUR FATHER

Our Father in heaven,
holy be your name,
your kingdom come and your will be done,
on earth as in heaven.
Give us today the kind of bread we need.
Forgive us our debts
just as we have forgiven those who are in debt to us.
Do not bring us to the test
but deliver us from the evil one.

CLOSING PRAYER

Most loving Father,
in the fight your Son waged, in the name of humanity,
against the forces of evil,
you made your benevolent plan triumph once and for all:
accord that I may be united to my Savior
when my hour comes to face death,
so that in him, I may pass from this world to you
and so be recognized by you as your beloved child.
Through Jesus Christ, your Son, our Savior,
in whom the elect will live with you,
in the communion of the Holy Spirit,
forever and ever.
Amen, amen, amen!

"Then the righteous
will shine like the sun
in the kingdom of their Father."

Jesus' Promise (Matthew 13:43)

AFTER YOUR RETREAT...

If you have enjoyed this retreat, and if you have found it beneficial with a view to the Kingdom of God, you can become a missionary for it:

- ▶ by speaking about it to others you know
- ▶ by witnessing to the graces you have received through it
- ▶ by giving this book as a gift
- ▶ by organizing group retreats within the framework of your parish or a community recognized by the Catholic Church

DIES IRAE

DIES IRAE
Giuseppe Verdi

THE *DIES IRAE* is a sequence which was traditionnaly sung before the Gospel during Requiem Masses. The version that has come down to us dates from the twelfth or thirteenth century. The inspiration for this supplication begins with the Book of Zephaniah and then becomes frankly apocalyptic. After the *Rex tremendae majestatis*, it draws inspiration from various parables regarding the Last Judgment found in the New Testament. The ending contains a direct reference to Matthew 25:31-48.

Verdi († 1901) composed his *Messa da Requiem* in memory of his very dear friend, the poet Alessandro Manzoni, who, like him, had fought for Italian unity during the *Risorgimento*. He was so distraught by Manzoni's death that he was unable to join his funeral cortège. Verdi considered this work, created in 1874, to be the crowning accomplishment of his career as a composer.

---

 39 minutes | Tracks 01 to 10

Dies iræ, dies illa,
Day of wrath and doom impending.

Solvet sæclum in favílla,
David's word with Sibyl's blending,

Teste David cum Sibýlla!
Heaven and earth in ashes ending.

Quantus tremor est futúrus,
Oh, what fear man's bosom rends,

quando judex est ventúrus,
when from heaven the Judge descends,

cuncta stricte discussúrus!
on whose sentence all depends.

BASS – CHOIR

Tuba mirum spargens sonum
Wondrous sound the trumpet flings;

per sepúlcra regiónum,
Through earth's sepulchres it rings;

coget omnes ante thronum.
All before the throne it brings.

BASS

Mors stupébit et Natúra,
Death is struck, and nature quaking,

cum resúrget creatúra,
All creation is awaking,

judicánti responsúra.
To its Judge an answer making.

MEZZO – CHOIR

Liber scriptus proferétur,
Lo, the book, exactly worded,

in quo totum continétur,
Wherein all hath been recorded,

unde Mundus judicétur.
Thence shall judgment be awarded.

Judex ergo cum sedébit,
When the Judge his seat attaineth,

quidquid latet apparébit,
And each hidden deed arraigneth,

nihil inúltum remanébit.
Nothing unavenged remaineth.

SOPRANO – MEZZO – TENOR

Quid sum miser tunc dictúrus?
What shall I, frail man, be pleading?

Quem patrónum rogatúrus,
Who for me be interceding,

cum vix justus sit secúrus?
When the just are mercy needing?

SOPRANO – MEZZO – TENOR
– BASS – CHOIR

Rex treméndæ majestátis,
King of Majesty tremendous,

qui salvándos salvas gratis,
Who does free salvation send us,

salva me, fons pietátis.
Fount of pity, then befriend us!

SOPRANO – MEZZO

Recordáre, Jesu pie,
Think, kind Jesus!—my salvation

quod sum causa tuæ viæ;
Caused Thy wondrous Incarnation;

ne me perdas illa die.
Leave me not to reprobation.

Quærens me, sedísti lassus,
Faint and weary, Thou hast sought me,

redemísti crucem passus,
On the Cross of suffering bought me.

tantus labor non sit cassus.
Shall such grace be vainly brought me?

Juste Judex ultiónis,
Righteous Judge, for sin's pollution

donum fac remissiónis
Grant Thy gift of absolution,

ante diem ratiónis.
Ere the day of retribution.

TENOR

Ingemísco, tamquam reus,
Guilty, now I pour my moaning,

culpa rubet vultus meus,
All my shame with anguish owning;

supplicánti parce Deus.
Spare, O God, Thy suppliant groaning!

Qui Maríam absolvísti,
Through the sinful woman shriven,

et latrónem exaudísti,
Through the dying thief forgiven,

mihi quoque spem dedísti.
Thou to me a hope hast given.

Preces meæ non sunt dignæ,
Worthless are my prayers and sighing,

sed tu bonus fac benígne,
Yet, good Lord, in grace complying,

ne perénni cremer igne.
Rescue me from fires undying.

Inter oves locum præsta,
With Thy favored sheep then place me,

et ab hædis me sequéstra,
Nor among the goats abase me,

státuens in parte dextra.
But to Thy right hand upraise me.

BASS – CHOIR

Confutátis maledíctis,
When the wicked are confounded,

flammis ácribus addíctis,
Doomed to flames of woe unbounded,

voca me cum benedíctis.
Call me with Thy saints surrounded.

Oro supplex et acclínis,
Low I kneel, with heart's submission,

cor contrítum quasi cinis,
See, like ashes, my contrition,

gere curam mei finis.
Help me in my last condition.

MEZZO – BASS – SOPRANO – TENOR – CHOIR

Lacrimósa dies illa,
Ah! that day of tears and mourning,

qua resúrget ex favílla
From the dust of earth returning

judicándus homo reus.
Man for judgement must prepare him,

Huic ergo parce, Deus.
Spare, O God, in mercy spare him.

Pie Jesu Dómine,
Lord, all-pitying, Jesus blest,

dona eis réquiem. Amen.
Grant them Thine eternal rest. Amen.

HOW TO ORGANIZE YOUR RETREAT

WHEN TO SCHEDULE YOUR RETREAT

Though the retreat requires less than an hour per day, it may be difficult for you to make time for it during a period of intense professional, familial, or volunteer activities.

So, if you work outside the home, or are a priest or religious, you should choose a time when your daily workload is relatively light. You could also wait to have time off to schedule your retreat, either at home or on vacation.

If you are staying home with children, you should choose a time when you know you will be able to have 30 to 40 minutes to yourself, away from your household, perhaps with the help of a friend or family member. You may also consider organizing the retreat as a Mother's Retreat at your parish, with scheduled childcare, for an hour each day.

FINDING THE RIGHT TIME OF DAY

At what time of day should you plan to do your retreat?

It all depends on your usual schedule.

Early birds may want to begin in the morning, an hour after breakfast. Night owls could, ideally, begin a couple of hours before bedtime.

But for just about everyone, other good times could be the hour before lunch, or (if you are on vacation) in the afternoon after a good nap.

Whatever your schedule looks like, you should choose your time according to one primary rule: you must be sure no one will disturb you—children or visitors, noise or activities that will distract your attention, etc.

Withdrawing yourself from the commotion and noise of the world is the primary meaning of the word "retreat."

You should also find some time—in the evening, for example—when you can look back over your notes and place yourself once again in the presence of the Mystery you have contemplated on that day.

BEING IN GOOD SHAPE

If you have eaten a big meal, if you have drunk alcohol, if you have slept badly, if you have watched a violent or stressful movie, etc., you can't expect to be able to concentrate on all the parts of the retreat and receive the desired benefit. So, once you've determined the schedule and timing of your retreat, you must be very attentive to your physical and spiritual health from the first day to the last.

On all seven (to ten) days of the retreat, it is indispensable to partially fast from media and entertainment. It will help you to develop the quality of your inner life.

If, despite a healthy diet and habits, on one day or another you don't feel in particularly good shape, before you begin, you might consider taking a 10-minute walk or a lukewarm shower, and then having a big glass of water or a cup of herbal tea.

CHOOSING THE RIGHT SETTING

If you can, you should always use the same place—preferably a quiet, peaceful room that isn't too bright. Don't hesitate to close the curtains, if necessary. As a general rule, avoid anything that excites or distracts the eye and thoughts; for example, avoid a window overlooking the street, a busy view, or a desk full of bills.

And, of course, turn off your landline and switch your cellphone to airplane mode.

If there are several people in the house, politely ask them to respect your retreat Hour every day for seven days—or ask them to take part in it with you.

You should sit at a small table, preferably facing a soberly decorated wall. Choose a good, comfortable chair. Beforehand, you should place on the table:

- ▶ this book, opened to the page of the day
- ▶ a crucifix or a cross
- ▶ a candle you will light to signal the beginning of the retreat Hour (please take all necessary precautions)
- ▶ a pen and a nice notepad to take notes
- ▶ a small bunch of fresh or dried flowers
- ▶ a large glass of water

Close to where you are praying, you might want to have a more comfortable armchair, sofa, or deckchair where you can sit and meditate—but you can also meditate just as well while remaining in your chair. If you prefer to sit on the floor to meditate, provide yourself with a comfortable little rug.

Also place audio equipment (good sound quality is essential) on the table, to listen to the music. Check before each session that the equipment is functioning properly, so you don't have to distract yourself unnecessarily as you are trying to play the correct track at the right time.

IN THE OUTDOORS?

It's not impossible to do your retreat outside. But, in that case, you will need to find a quiet, calm, isolated spot where you are sure you won't be disturbed, even by flies or mosquitoes!

In addition, your spot should be well-shaded, as full daylight is not conducive to the inner life. As El Greco, a painter of the Spanish Renaissance, once said, "I never go out before 6 p.m., in order to protect my internal light from the sunlight." You should also not sit in front of a beautiful view; this would be a distraction. In any event, have an alternate, indoor plan ready, in case of rain or high winds.

RELAX AND FOCUS

Before entering into the retreat, you should begin with a short time of relaxation.

- ▶ Sit on the chair with your feet flat on the ground and your hands on your thighs or knees, in such a way that your legs, arms, and back are in a natural, comfortable position.
- ▶ Let your head drop slightly toward your chest.
- ▶ Close your eyes and breathe slowly and calmly, gradually prolonging each breath as you inhale, then each breath as you exhale. Each breath you exhale should last twice as long as each breath you inhale.
- ▶ When you get to the point that each breath you inhale is slow and calm, begin a cycle of exercises: inhale deeply, really filling your lungs, and pause 3 or 4 seconds. Then slowly and calmly exhale; when your lungs are empty, pause for 3 or 4 seconds. Begin the full cycle again: inhale completely/pause/exhale completely/pause. Repeat this 10 times.

✻ *N.B.* Be aware that this exercise, and above all the pauses, should never get to the point of causing the slightest discomfort, and certainly not any anxiety. Should that happen, stop the exercise. After relaxing for a moment, you can begin again, inhaling and exhaling a little less deeply, and pausing for a shorter time.

MAINTAINING YOUR CONCENTRATION

During the Hour, you must take care not to let your mind wander or stray into daydreams. That would spoil at once all the efforts you have made to develop your concentration. Listening to music, reading, reciting a prayer should signal to the mind and the heart: "Mandatory focus on what I'm listening to, what I'm reading, and what I'm saying in prayer! Exit forbidden!" As an exception, you could authorize your mind to wander for a few minutes at the end of the meditation, but that's all.

....

WHAT TO DO WHEN YOU CATCH YOUR MIND WANDERING

....

Take a break and have a time-out from the Hour.

First, make yourself fully aware again of the personal goal you set for yourself when you decided to make this retreat. To do so, you could ask yourself the following questions: Do you want to spend your time in daydreams that lead you off in all directions? Or do you want to make a retreat that, while demanding, will lead you to heights that can only be attained by respecting the rules, as in mountain climbing?

Second, think deeply about what awaits you if you carry out your retreat to the end: the joy of the climb, the discovery of vistas you did not know existed, the wonder of arriving at the summit and of feeling that you have been transported beyond yourself... That's well worth putting in the extra effort.

Third, trace back to the exact point when you lost concentration and use a pencil to mark it with a cross in your book. If something you did not understand caused your mind to wander, return to this difficulty and reflect on it a little more rather than skipping over it. If that isn't the case, continue the course of the retreat, but mark a cross at a passage each time your attention slips. If you have more than three crosses in the same section, you should take a break rather than continuing (unless you're near the end of the Hour). Stop for a quarter of an hour, get some air, go for a little walk, have a cup of coffee or tea or a large glass of water. Then start again at the beginning of the section where you left off.

AUDIO CREDITS

CD 1

TRACK 1 – DIES IRAE – 02:18
"Verdi: Messa da Requiem: II. Sequence, 1. Dies Irae (Chorus)"

TRACK 2 – TUBA MIRUM – 01:59
"Verdi: Messa da Requiem: II. Sequence, 2. Tuba mirum (Chorus)"

TRACK 3 – MORS STUPEBIT – 01:36
"Verdi: Messa da Requiem: II. Sequence, 3. Mors stupebit (Bass)"

TRACK 4 – LIBER SCRIPTUS – 05:14
"Verdi: Messa da Requiem: II. Sequence, 4. Liber scriptus. Dies Irae (Mezzo-soprano, Chorus)"

TRACK 5 – QUID SUM MISER – 03:48
"Verdi: Messa da Requiem: II. Sequence, 5. Quid sum miser (Soprano, Mezzo-soprano, Tenor)"

TRACK 6 – REX TREMENDAE – 03:53
"Verdi: Messa da Requiem: II. Sequence, 6. Rex tremendae (Chorus, Soprano, Mezzo-soprano, Tenor, Bass)"

TRACK 7 – RECORDARE – 04:16
"Verdi: Messa da Requiem: II. Sequence, 7. Recordare (Soprano, Mezzo-soprano)"

TRACK 8 – INGEMISCO – 03:43
"Verdi: Messa da Requiem: II. Sequence, 8. Ingemisco (Tenor)"

TRACK 9 – CONFUTATIS – 05:38
"Verdi: Messa da Requiem: II. Sequence, 9. Confutatis. Dies Irae (Bass, Chorus)"

TRACK 10 – LACRYMOSA – 06:28
"Verdi: Messa da Requiem: II. Sequence, 10. Lacrymosa (Mezzo-soprano, Bass, Soprano, Tenor, Chorus)"

For tracks 1 to 10: Giuseppe Verdi (1813-1901) – Cheryl Studer, Soprano – Dolora Zajick, Mezzo-soprano – Luciano Pavarotti, Tenor – Samuel Ramey, Bass – Coro e Orchestra del Teatro alla Scala, Milano, Chorus. Direction: Riccardo Muti. With the kind permission of Warner Music France, a Warner Music Group Company. ℗ 1987 Warner Classics / Warner Music UK Ltd, a Warner Music Group Company.

TRACK 11 – MISERERE MEI, DEUS – 11:59
Compositor: Gregorio Allegri – Ensemble Tenebrae – Direction: Nigel Short ℗ Signum Classics.

TRACK 12 – VENI SANCTE SPIRITUS – 02:46
"Veni sancte spiritus, Sequence, Mode I" – Coro de Monjes del Monasterio de Silos.
With the kind permission of Warner Music France, a Warner Music Group Company. ℗ 1980 Warner Music Spain, S.L., a Warner Music Group Company.

TRACK 13 – CHORUS OF THE HEBREW SLAVES (VA PIENSERO) – 05:12
"Verdi: Nabucco, Act 3: 'Va, pensiero, sull'ali dorate' (Chorus)" – Giuseppe Verdi (1813-1901) – Philharmonia Orchestra & Ambrosian Opera Chorus. Direction: Riccardo Muti.
With the kind permission of Warner Music France, a Warner Music Group Company.
℗ 1986 Warner Classics / Warner Music UK Ltd, a Warner Music Group Company.

TRACK 14 – RORATE CAELI DESUPER – 05:01
"'Rorate Caeli desuper' – Preces, Modo I" – Benedictine Monks Choir of Santo Domingo de Silos ℗ & © 1995 – 2004 – 2009 Éditions Jade – With the kind permission of ÉDITIONS JADE.

CD 2

TRACK 1 – MAGNIFICAT – 05:26
"Magnificat sexti toni" – Adrian Willaert (1490-1562) – Oxford Camerata – Direction: Jeremy Summerly. ℗ Naxos Rights US, Inc. represented by Kapagama Classique.

TRACK 2 – CANTICLE OF BEATITUDES – 02:43
"Troisième antienne : Les Béatitudes" – Ensemble Harmonie Géorgienne – Direction: Nana Peradze ℗ 2013 Nana Peradze – © 2013 Nana Peradze / Éditions Jade – With the kind permission of ÉDITIONS JADE.

TRACK 3 – THIRD LESSON OF TENEBRAE – 12:48
François Couperin (1668-1733) – Montserrat Figueras, soprano – Maria Cristina Kiehr, soprano – Rolf Lislevand, theorbo – Pierre Hantaï, harpsichord – Jordi Savall, viola de gamba ℗ 1991, Alia Vox.

TRACK 4 – STABAT MATER – 13:02
"Stabat Mater pour les Religieuses" – Marc-Antoine Charpentier (1643-1704) – La Capella Reial de Catalunya – Le Concert des Nations – Direction: Jordi Savall ℗ 1991, Alia Vox.

Page 69: *Christ and the Apostles (I am the Vine),* Greek School, 17ᵗʰ c., tempera on panel, 13.8 x 15.4 in., Byzantine Museum, Athens (Greece). © Bridgeman Images.

Page 71: *Moses Exposed* (detail), Gustave Moreau (Paris, 1826 – Paris, 1898), oil on canvas, 31.9 x 39.4 in., Gustave Moreau Museum, Paris (France). © RMN-GP / Christian Jean.

Page 72-73: Wall, Pompeii (Italy). © Petr Svarc / Alamy Banque d'Images.

Page 74: *The Family* (1886), John Dickson Batten (Plymouth, 1860-1932), oil on canvas, 50 x 40.2 in., Collection of Fred and Sherry Ross, Art Renewal Center, Port Reading (N.J., USA). © Image courtesy of the Art Renewal Center® www.artrenewal.org.

Page 77: *The Visitation* (detail, c. 1310-1320), Master Heinrich of Constance (14ᵗʰ c.), wood, 23.2 x 11.9 x 7.2 in., Metropolitan Museum of Art, New York City (N.Y., USA). Photo: Public Domain.

Page 79: *The Childhood of the Virgin* (c. 1658), Francisco de Zurbarán (Fuente de Cantos, 1598 – Madrid, 1664), oil on canvas, 29 x 21 in., State Hermitage Museum, St. Petersburg (Russia). © Bridgeman Images.

Page 82: *The Virgin with Child* (detail, 1900), William-Adolphe Bouguereau (La Rochelle, 1825 – La Rochelle, 1905), oil on canvas, 112.2 x 72.8 in., Petit Palais Museum, Paris (France). © FineArtImages / Leemage.

Page 89: *Mother and Child* (c. 1903), George Frederic Watts (London, 1817 – Compton, Surrey, 1904), oil on canvas, 30 x 25 in., Watts Gallery, Compton, Surrey (UK). © Trustees of Watts Gallery / Bridgeman Images.

Page 91: *Nativity,* Gentile da Fabriano (Fabriano, c. 1370 – Rome, 1427), tempera on wood, 28.4 x 16.8 in., The J. Paul Getty Museum, Los Angeles (CA., USA). Photo: Digital Image, courtesy of the Getty's Open Program.

Page 93: *The Heavenly and Earthly Trinities* (c. 1681), Bartolomé Esteban Murillo (Séville, 1617 – Séville, 1682), oil on canvas, 115.3 x 81.5 in., National Gallery, London (UK). © The National Gallery, London / akg-images.

Page 95: *The Good Shepherd,* fresco from the Catacombs of Priscilla, 3ʳᵈ c., Rome (Italy). © Aisa / Leemage.

Page 96: *The Crucifixion,* Bronzino (Florence, 1503 – Florence, 1572), oil on wood, 57 x 45.3 in., Museum of Fine Arts, Nice (France). © Nice, musée Musée des Beaux-Arts.

Page 102: *The Face of Christ* (1649), Claude Mellan (Abbeville, 1598 – Paris, 1688), oil on canvas, 9 x 11 in., Private Collection.

Page 107: *The Virgin Supported by Saint John, from a Crucifixion Group,* ca. 1340–50, Belgium, Marble, traces of gilding, 22 3/16 x 8 7/8 x 4 1/4 in. New York, Metropolitan Museum. Photo: Public Domain.

Page 111: *Pietà,* Daniele Crespi (Busto Arsizio, 1598 – Milan, 1630), oil on canvas, 60.6 x 50.4 in., Prado Museum, Madrid (Spain). © Dist. RMN-GP / image du Prado.

Page 113: *Crucifixion of Christ* (detail, c. 1632), Diego Velázquez (Seville, 1599 – Madrid, 1660), oil on canvas, 97.6 x 66.5 in., Prado Museum, Madrid (Spain). © Dist. RMN-GP / image du Prado.

Page 114: *The Resurrection of Christ* (1639), Rembrandt (Leyde, 1606 – Amsterdam, 1669), oil on canvas, 36.2 x 26.4 in., Alte Pinakothek, Munich (Germany). © akg-images / André Held.

Page 122: *Risen Christ* (c. 1600), South Germany, gilt bronze, 9.4 in. © The Cecil Beaton Studio Archive at Sotheby's.

Page 124: *Christ at Emmaus* (detail, 1648), Rembrandt (Leyde, 1606 – Amsterdam, 1669), oil on canvas, 26.8 x 25.6 in., Louvre Museum, Paris (France). © RMN-GP / Philippe Fuzeau.

Page 127: *Ecce Homo and the Mourning Virgin* (detail, c. 1530-1540), Adriaen Isenbrant (Bruges, 1490 – Bruges, 1551), oil on canvas, 41.5 x 36.5 in., Metropolitan Museum of Art, New York City (N.Y., USA). Photo: Public Domain.

Page 133: *The Faith* (1522), Andrea del Sarto (Florence, 1486 – Florence, 1531), fresco, 76.4 x 43.3 in., Chiostro dello Scalzo, Florence (Italy). © Luisa Ricciarini / Bridgeman Images.

TEXT CREDITS